BECOM
Law Professor

A Candidate's Guide

Brannon P. Denning

Marcia L. McCormick

Jeffrey M. Lipshaw

Foreword by Lawrence Solum

AMERICAN BAR ASSOCIATION
Defending Liberty
Pursuing Justice

Cover design by ABA Publishing.

The materials contained herein represent the opinions and views of the authors and/or the editors, and should not be construed to be the views or opinions of the law firms or companies with whom such persons are in partnership with, associated with, or employed by, nor of the American Bar Association, unless adopted pursuant to the bylaws of the Association.

Nothing contained in this book is to be considered as the rendering of legal advice, either generally or in connection with any specific issue or case. Readers are responsible for obtaining advice from their own lawyers or other professionals. This book and any forms and agreements herein are intended for educational and informational purposes only.

Printed in the United States of America.

14 13 12 11   5 4 3 2

Library of Congress Cataloging-in-Publication Data

Denning, Brannon P.
  Becoming a law professor: a candidate's guide / by Brannon P. Denning,
Marcia L. McCormick, Jeffrey M. Lipshaw. — 1st ed.
    p. cm.
  Includes bibliographical references and index.
  ISBN 978-1-60442-994-7
  1. Law teachers—Vocational guidance—United States. 2. Law—United
States—Study and teaching. 3. Law schools—United States—Employees. I.
McCormick, Marcia. II. Lipshaw, Jeffrey M. III. Title.
  KF272.D46 2010
  340.071'173—dc22

                                                                    2010042094

Discounts are available for books ordered in bulk. Special consideration is given to state bars, CLE programs, and other bar-related organizations. Inquire at Book Publishing, ABA Publishing, American Bar Association, 321 North Clark Street, Chicago, Illinois 60654-7598.

www.ababooks.org

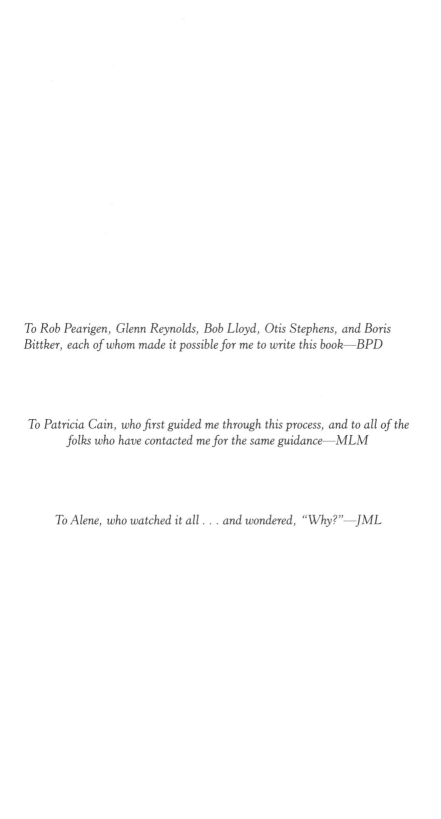

To Rob Pearigen, Glenn Reynolds, Bob Lloyd, Otis Stephens, and Boris Bittker, each of whom made it possible for me to write this book—BPD

To Patricia Cain, who first guided me through this process, and to all of the folks who have contacted me for the same guidance—MLM

To Alene, who watched it all . . . and wondered, "Why?"—JML

CONTENTS

Becoming a Law Professor began as an office conversation between Denning and McCormick. We were soon joined by Lipshaw, who had been thinking about a similar project after the runaway success of his article "How Not to Retire and Teach." The three of us have had a lot of fun writing this book, and hope that it will prove as useful to present and future candidates as it was enjoyable to write.

This book would not have been possible without the contribution and support of a number of people who thought that a book like this would be useful and who encouraged us to write it. In June of 2007, Denning guest-blogged at *Concurring Opinions* and mentioned that he was working on the book. A number of people gave thoughtful responses to his "bleg"* asking what ought to be included in the book. Not all the suggestions were signed, but we want to thank everyone who responded, including Bruce Boyden, Andy Grewal, James Grimmelman, David Hardy, Orin Kerr, Sarah Lawsky, and Robert Rhee.

Special thanks are owed to Ben Barton, Beth Burch, Miriam Cherry, Chad Flanders, Orly Lobel, Dan Markel, Bill Ross, Christina Sautter, Larry Solum, Brad Wendel, Chuck Young, and the anonymous reviewers at the ABA, each of whom read early drafts in their entirety and made extremely helpful suggestions for improving the final draft. Thanks, too, to Stephen Gidiere for putting us in touch with the right folks at ABA Publishing and to Rick Paszkiet for persuading his colleagues that a market existed for such a book.

The authors also thank Monica Nelson, Elizabeth Barclay, and Charlie Nelson, each of whom provided valuable research assistance on the book, including compiling and updating the bibliographic essay in Appendix A. Pam Davis and Donna Klosowsky were invaluable in preparing the manuscript.

Denning wishes to thank Dean John Carroll and the Cumberland School of Law for successive summer research grants that aided in the completion of this book. As always, he is humbled by and grateful for the constant love and support from Alli, Gram, and Meg.

McCormick wishes to thank the faculty at Chicago-Kent for helping to launch this part of her career during her time there as a VAP, particularly Marty Malin, Mary Rose Strubbe, and Katharine Baker. For the endless conversations about this topic, thanks to fellow VAPs Kari Aamot, Mark Bauer, Mike Cahill, Molly Current, Beth Henning, Joe Morrissey, Kristen Osenga, Mike Pardo, Greg Pingree, and Alex Tsesis, and non-VAPs Deb Cohen and Paul Secunda. Thanks to Dean John Carroll and the faculty at Cumberland School of Law for allowing her to see the other side of hiring. And finally, thanks to John, Morgan, Ceridwen, Rhiannon, Mark, Marla, Victoria, and everyone from Book Club, none of whom have ever doubted, even when she has.

ACKNOWLEDGMENTS

---

* to write a blog entry for the sole purpose of asking for something.

Lipshaw wishes to thank Andy Klein and Brad Wendel for suggesting that the twenty "humorous" dos and don'ts ought to be an essay about not retiring and teaching, and Brannon and Marcia for including him in this project.

Brannon P. Denning
Birmingham, Alabama

Marcia L. McCormick
St. Louis, Missouri

Jeffrey M. Lipshaw
Boston, Massachusetts

The New Realities of the Legal Academy

Lawrence B. Solum*

Brannon P. Denning, Marcia L. McCormick, and Jeffrey M. Lipshaw have done the legal academy a great service by writing *Becoming a Law Professor: A Candidate's Guide*. This is a soup-to-nuts guide, taking aspiring legal academics from their first aspirations on a step-by-step journey through the practicalities of the Association of American Law School's hiring conference, on-campus interviews, and preparing for the first semester of teaching. Although the blogosphere is filled with advice and many helpful articles have been written about the process of becoming a law professor, there is nothing comparable to *Becoming a Law Professor*—which is sure to become essential reading for anyone seeking a job as a legal academic.

One of the great virtues of Denning, McCormick, and Lipshaw's guide is that it reflects the changing nature and new realities of the legal academy. Not so many years ago, entry into the elite legal academy was mostly a function of two things—credentials and connections. The ideal candidate graduated near the top of the class at a top-five law school, held an important editorial position on law review, clerked for a Supreme Court Justice, and practiced for a few years at an elite firm or government agency in New York or Washington. Credentials like these almost guaranteed a job at a very respectable law school, but the very best jobs went to those with connections—the few who were held in high esteem by the elite network of very successful legal academics and their friends in the bar and on the bench. The not-so-elite legal academy operated by a similar set of rules. Regional law schools were populated by a mix of graduates from elite schools and the top graduates of local schools, clerks of respected local judges, and alumni of elite law firms in the neighborhood. In what we now call the "bad old days," it was very difficult indeed for someone to become a law professor without glowing credentials and the right connections.

But times have changed. When the Association of American Law Schools created the annual Faculty Recruitment Conference (FRC) and the associated Faculty Appointments Register (FAR), the landscape of the legal

* Lawrence B. Solum is the John E. Cribbet Professor of Law and Professor of Philosophy at the University of Illinois.

academy was forever changed. The change was slow in coming. For many years, candidates were selected for interviews at the FRC on the basis of the same old credentials and connections, but at some point (many would say the early 1980s), the rules of the game began to change. In baseball, a similar change is associated with Billy Beane, the manager of the Oakland Athletics, who defied conventional wisdom and built winning teams despite severe financial constraints by relying on statistically reliable predictors of success.[1] The corresponding insight in the legal academy (developed by hiring committees at several law schools) was that the best predictor of success as a legal scholar was a record of publication. It turns out that law school grades, law review offices, and clerkships are at best very rough indicators of scholarly success. But those who successfully publish high-quality legal scholarship are likely to continue to do so.

The emergence of so-called "moneyball" hiring in the legal academy is good news for some aspiring legal academics and not so good news for others. If they learn nothing else, readers of Denning, McCormick, and Lipshaw's guide will surely learn this: Even if you are not a Supreme Court clerk, the editor of the *Yale Law Journal*, or even the graduate of a top-twenty law school, you can get a good job at an American law school with a rich intellectual environment. Even today, if you have the right connections and credentials, you are likely to be given a chance at an elite law school, but the best jobs will go to those with more than just credentials and connections. Whatever law school you have attended, whether or not you have clerked, and whatever job you took after law school, the new reality of the legal academy is that your ability to produce excellent legal scholarship will determine how far your connections and credentials (or lack thereof) will take you.

This transformation has multiple manifestations, but two developments illustrate the profound nature of the change. Here is a fact that some may find startling. It is no longer clear that a Supreme Court clerkship is the magic key to the door of the legal academy. Indeed, many of the savviest players in the law-school hiring game do not even view a stint on the Supreme Court as a substantial plus factor; a few view it as a negative. Here is another fact that has increasingly become common knowledge: The credentials of many entry-level candidates today would have qualified their possessors for tenure at almost any elite American law school two or three decades ago.

The new realities of the legal academy are connected with intellectual history of legal scholarship in the United States. Since the rise of American legal realism, it has been clear that the best legal scholarship involved more

---

1. Beane's exploits were described by Michael Lewis in his book *Moneyball: The Art of Winning an Unfair Game* (2003).

than descriptive doctrinal scholarship. Beginning with the rise of the law-and-economics and law-and-society movements in the 1950s and 1960s, interdisciplinarity has become increasingly important in legal scholarship. For decades now, the best legal scholarship has answered the question, "What should the law be?" Lawyers are trained to answer the question, "What is the law?" The tools suited to that task (case crunching, code crunching, and clause crunching) are the central focus of the core curriculum of American law schools. The normative turn in legal scholarship has required legal academics to acquire new tools—from economics, philosophy, sociology, political science, history, and elsewhere. But these new tools, the bread and butter of the legal academic, are not the explicit focus of the standard law-school course—which focuses almost exclusively on primary legal materials (cases, statutes, regulations, rules, and constitutions) and rarely (indeed, almost never) includes a systematic introduction to the canon of legal scholarship.

So the aspiring legal academic faces an exhilarating but daunting task. Preparing for the academic job market requires the candidate to accomplish two tasks. The most obvious task is the development of a portfolio of scholarship—the proverbial three articles to be listed in the three spaces provided on the form submitted for the Association of American Law School's Faculty Appointments Register. But the most important task—both for getting your first job and for long-term success in the legal academy—is the acquisition of the tools and knowledge that form the groundwork for excellent legal scholarship. Both tasks require time! Because law school (even in the elite legal academy) is focused on preparation for the practice of law, it is increasingly common for the candidates for jobs in the legal academy to pursue an advanced degree (a Ph.D. in another discipline, an LL.M., or an advanced doctorate in law) and the legal equivalent of a postdoctoral experience, usually in the form of a fellowship or visiting assistant professorship. One year of intensive preparation for the academic job market may be sufficient, although these days two is increasingly the norm and three is not uncommon.

Whatever your background, however high or low your ambitions, and whenever you make the decision to seek a job in the legal academy, one of your first steps should be to read *Becoming a Law Professor: A Candidate's Guide* and the resources to which it points. If you are reading this foreword, you have undoubtedly heard that the job of law professor is frequently called "the best job on earth." That may be an exaggeration, but there is surely a kernel of truth in the aphorism. But if law professors have great jobs, they are not easy jobs—not easy to get and increasingly not easy to keep. Like Brannon P. Denning, Marcia L. McCormick, and Jeffrey M. Lipshaw, I wish you every success on the hard road you have chosen. Their sage advice will surely help you to anticipate the twists and turns on the road to becoming a law professor.

If your first law review article was published in the *Harvard Law Review* or the *Yale Law Journal*; if Cass Sunstein, Richard Posner, Ronald Dworkin, Kathleen Sullivan, or Elena Kagan is making phone calls to appointments committee chairs on your behalf; or if you are presently a clerk for a justice of the Supreme Court of the United States, congratulations, professor, you'll do just fine when you decide to enter the academy. When we started this project, we had the idea that as long as a person graduated from one of the ten or eleven law schools that produce roughly seventy percent of law teachers each year,[2] was on law review, and clerked for a federal judge, that person was a shoo-in for an academic career or at least knew that he or she could be an academic and knew how to pursue that career path. Thus, we originally conceived of this project as a guide to becoming a law professor the hard way,[3] designed for those who may have had mediocre grades in the first year, did not do moot court or were not on law review, did not clerk for a federal judge, and, most of all, did not graduate from one of those eleven law schools. After talking to a number of our colleagues, we came to the conclusion (if our sample was typical) that the great majority of current law professors, even ones who graduated from Harvard, Yale, or Stanford, felt their path was plenty hard and had to work to figure out the process and to get a teaching job. So if you can be reached by calling (202) 479-3000,[4] you are excused, but for everybody else who has thought about being a law professor, this is the book for you!

We are writing this book to provide information to, and encourage, more law school students to approach academia as a realistic career choice. We believe that non-Order of the Coif, non-law review, and even non-Ivy League graduates can become excellent teachers and scholars, and that legal academia in general would be enhanced by the presence in significant numbers of professors who possess a diversity of academic backgrounds and experiences. Unfortunately, many people who would be fantastic teachers and scholars never even consider teaching as an option. In part, this is because of students' assumptions (unfortunately often perpetuated by faculty) that even if you are at the top of your class at Non-Ivy-Equivalent-State-Law-School your chances at successfully obtaining employment in the academy are nil. But we also think that the relative lack of information about teaching and the hiring market tends to reinforce such perceptions and discourages students from pursuing academic opportunities. Even at Ivy League law schools, the lore surrounding the academic market was sometimes passed on selectively by professors to favored students. This book seeks to make such information available to everyone.

---

2. *See, e.g.*, Lawrence B. Solum, *Entry-Level Hiring Reports*, LEGAL THEORY BLOG, http://lsolum.typepad.com/legaltheory/2010/04/entry-level-hiring-survey-2010.html (Apr. 12, 2010). Professor Solum conducts an entry-level hiring survey each spring. The 2010 results may reflect fewer absolute numbers than usual (probably the result of the 2008–09 financial crisis), but the percentages have stayed about the same. The survey reported 101 entry-level hires at American law schools, of which seventy came from Yale, Harvard, NYU, Columbia, Virginia, Berkeley, Penn, Chicago, Michigan, and Stanford.

3. Indeed, our working title for the book was "Becoming a Law Professor the Hard Way."

4. The main phone number of the Supreme Court of the United States.

Make no mistake: The hiring market for law professors—even candidates who graduated from top law schools—is extremely competitive. In 2008–09, a total of 875 people filled out resumes for the Association of American Law Schools' Faculty Appointments Register (about which more later);[5] roughly 150 received offers from law schools. Moreover, the job itself is often more demanding than many candidates expect, as new faculty members often find out. It is not for everyone. We know of a few people who, after teaching, decided to go back into private practice. Most law professors, however, would not trade their jobs for any other. If you think that you might be one of those people, we encourage you to read this book and use what we learned through our experiences to aid you in the sometimes long, sometimes arduous process of becoming a candidate and, one hopes, a successful candidate.

Our book is organized in the following way. Chapter 1 describes the types of teaching jobs available in law schools and the responsibilities of each. As you will see, not everyone on a law school faculty teaches two courses a semester and writes 1.5 law review articles a year. Chapter 2 then describes possible paths to teaching, from the "standard model" law professor to various alternative paths that many current professors (including the authors) have taken instead. While we describe the standard model in detail, we do so mostly to contrast it with the various "hard ways" that one might take to get to the academy.

Chapters 3 through 6 constitute the "how-to" of the book. We describe in detail the law school hiring process from application through the AALS "meat market" to the on-campus visit and the job offer. We include a special chapter (chapter 5) offering advice to nontraditional job candidates of all sorts about handling issues that may come up during the interview process.

In chapter 7 we offer some advice for the new professor. We do not intend for this to be a book about successful teaching—there is at least one good book and a number of articles on that subject[6]—but there are things that professor-designates ought to think about between the time the offer is accepted and the first class is taught. Much in this chapter is drawn from our personal experience and that of our colleagues; it is of the "I wish I'd thought of that" variety.

We conclude, in chapter 8, with some suggestions in the event your first foray into the academic job market fails to produce an offer. Each of us went through the process more than once; we discovered that even an unsuccessful initial search can yield opportunities that will aid future searches.

We also include an annotated bibliography of articles on the hiring process and other aspects of becoming a law professor, as well as a brief primer on the law review submissions process. Throughout the chapters, we've included

---

5. For the AALS registration figures, see *2008-09 AALS Statistical Report on Law Faculty*, http://www.aals.org/statistics/2009far/registration.html. The estimate on actual hires for that year comes from Professor Solum's 2009 database. Lawrence B. Solum, *Entry-Level Hiring Reports*, LEGAL THEORY BLOG, http://lsolum.typepad.com/legaltheory/2009/04/2009-entry-level-hiring-report.html (Apr. 26, 2009).

6. *See, e.g.*, Madeleine Schachter, *The Law Professor's Handbook: A Practical Guide to Teaching Law* (2004); Mary Olszewska & Thomas E. Baker, *An Annotated Bibliography on Law Teaching*, http://papers.ssrn.com/sol3/papers.cfm?abstract_id=1497031.

sidebars from us and from friends and colleagues offering narrative accounts of their own job searches. We thought these voices would humanize and particularize the general accounts we offer in the chapter. We have also included timelines and checklists at the end of some chapters for readers who might find such organizational tools helpful.

In addition to our primary aim—to collect in a single place information about legal academia and the law school hiring process—we hope that this book might encourage law schools and their hiring committees to look beyond the usual suspects at the AALS and consider folks, like us, who entered teaching through nontraditional routes. Perhaps what we write here might even start a conversation about intellectual and educational diversity within law faculties. Broadening candidate pools and critically evaluating the tendency toward credentialism in hiring will, we firmly believe, benefit both institutions and students in the long run.[7] We also hope that our book will find its way into the hands of career service personnel at schools not known for producing professors, if only to suggest it to the right students as a possible alternative to practice.

We wish you the very best of luck in your pursuits and sincerely hope we can help. If you find our book helpful, or if you have suggestions for possible future editions, we would love to hear from you! You can reach us at our respective institutions, or contact us by e-mail at bpdennin@samford.edu; mmccor20@slu.edu; or jlipshaw@suffolk.edu.

---

7. That's not to say there's no conversation going on presently about the future of the legal academy. *See, e.g.,* Pierre Schlag, *Spam Jurisprudence, Air Law, and the Rank Anxiety of Nothing Happening (A Report on the State of the Art),* 97 GEO. L.J. 803 (2009); Richard A. Posner, *The State of Legal Scholarship Today: A Comment on Schlag,* 97 GEO. L.J. 845 (2009). "Hard way" candidates ought to be encouraged by thoughts such as this one, coming from Frank Wu, the dean of the University of California—Hastings School of Law:

> While it is better that those of us whose research cross over into other fields (as mine does) are trained formally, rather than dilettantes (as I am), I have a concern that we will see this new breed of law professor not as one of many valuable types an institution should recruit and nurture but rather as the best and the only type that matters—to the exclusion of those with substantial practice experience, those who would teach in clinical programs, and those who produce the sort of doctrinal analysis that was perfectly respectable a generation ago and valuable to judges and lawyers today still. It does a disservice to our students, among others, if we become so enamored with our own speculations and engrossed in impressing one another with our citations to Wittgenstein (and, yes, I know enough about Wittgenstein to distinguish between the earlier and the later) that we forget we earn our keep by training individuals who by and large become advocates and counselors for causes and clients. Some of us should do work that is of greater interest to sociologists, but some of us also should do work that is of greater interest to the bench and the bar; others of us will try our best to do a little of each. These are all worthwhile contributions.

Frank Wu, *Who Could Be Hired Today,* CONCURRING OPINIONS (Apr. 4, 2009), http://www.concurringopinions.com/archives/2009/04/who_could_be_hi.html#more.

What Do Law Professors Do All Day?

Like Caesar's Gaul, the job of a law professor has three parts: teaching, scholarship, and service. As we'll see in this chapter, some law professors' jobs are heavily weighted to one or more of those parts. Some schools, for example, reward the production of scholarship to the near-exclusion of the other two. Other schools might stress teaching or service, weighing both more than, or at least as much as, scholarship. Whatever valence is given to each component, it should be clear by the end of this chapter that law professors do not simply cruise into school once or twice a week to teach for a couple of hours, head out to collect hefty consulting fees, then retire to their palatial homes for a round of golf and a scotch. (Although, if you know how to find that job, please contact the authors.)

Law professors occupy (we think) a relatively unique position between, on one hand, practicing lawyers, and on the other, professors in other social science and humanities disciplines. Indeed, we suspect the foregoing description of the life of the law professor is what springs to mind every time a long-time practitioner murmurs wistfully, "I think I'd like to retire and teach." To the long-time law professor, that sentiment, when actually uttered by those aspiring to enter the academy, is the ultimate disrespect, but one with a rich if not proud history. There are more thorough sources on the development of the legal academy since C.C. Langdell wrought his case method revolution,[1] but it is fair to say for our purposes that law as academic discipline still bears some of the neuroses that arose in its difficult childhood and adolescence, growing as it did from trade school roots to its present ranks in the forefront of first-tier research universities.

---

1. Though not all schools are on board with the recommendations contained therein, anybody looking to enter the legal academy would do well to read the MacCrate Report and the Carnegie Report on legal education. *See* Robert MacCrate, ed.,*Legal Education and Professional Development—An Educational Continuum* (1992); William M. Sullivan et al. eds., *Educating Lawyers: Preparation for the Profession of Law* (2007). For an historical perspective on American legal education, see William P. Lapiana, *Logic and Experience: The Origin of Modern American Legal Education* (1994); Robert Stevens, *Law School: Legal Education in America from the 1850s to the 1980s* (1983); Thomas F. Bergin, *Law Teacher: A Man Divided Against Himself*, 54 VA. L. REV. 637 (1968).

So while practicing lawyers may imagine that their academic counterparts live lives of comparative ease, having broken free of the surly bonds of billable hours, academic lawyers still often see themselves as catching up with their academic colleagues, not so much as teachers but as scholars. Consider, for example, that the lowliest assistant professor in the philosophy department has received a Ph.D., and has therefore already produced a book-length, peer-reviewed dissertation, which the professor has defended in the oral examination. On the other hand, the teaching degree in law has, historically at least, been the same one as the practice degree. To take history as an example, graduate schools in the humanities do not generally turn out professional history practitioners like, say, Doris Kearns Goodwin, David McCullough, or Steven Ambrose. Historians, by and large, are scholars, and don't "practice" history. Academic historians don't have to worry about highly paid "tradespeople" invading their turf. At the other extreme, while academic physicians often don't make what their private practice counterparts make, universities run big teaching hospitals in which academics teach, research, and still practice medicine. (This model is replicated to a limited extent in law schools' clinics, in which students represent low-income clients in civil or criminal matters.) While we don't vouch for this casual social psychology, we can certainly understand why academic lawyers look for ways to distinguish themselves from their equivalently degreed practitioner peers.

The opposite side of this coin is that academic law, in addition to wanting to distinguish itself from the "fish" of ordinary practitioners, wants to integrate itself more fully with the "fowl" of research-oriented humanities and physical and social sciences. Thirty years ago, and certainly fifty years ago, the great legal scholars produced the great treatises on legal doctrine—Williston and Corbin on contracts, Prosser on torts, Wright and Miller on the Federal Rules of Civil Procedure, for example. Though legal scholars continue to produce fine scholarship on doctrinal and legal policy matters, "law and X," where "X" equals another discipline like economics, or political theory, or evolutionary biology, or philosophy, is the hallmark of the present legal academy. To get a sense of this, skim through fifty or so of the most recent "law articles" posted on SSRN. [2] Where thirty years ago, the overwhelming majority of new legal professors had only the J.D. (or LL.B.) as their graduate degree, in excess of 40 percent of the candidates for jobs in the 2008–2009 academic year had either an advanced law degree or an advanced degree in another discipline.[3]

Similarly, law schools have an employment structure that reflects how colleges and universities, not law firms and businesses, govern themselves. They are run in large part by deans and by faculties themselves. Law faculties

---

2. SSRN, the Social Science Research Network, is a database that includes thousands of articles posted in real-time by legal and finance scholars all over the world. If you have never looked at it, type the URL http://ssrn.com into the address bar of your browser. If you have never read a law professor blog, start doing it now. If there is an Association of American Law Schools (AALS) Listserv in your area, try to join it.

3. *2008–2009 AALS Statistical Report on Law Faculty*, http://www.aals.org/statistics/2009far/degrees.html.

are a bit like families, with some of the shared responsibilities and dysfunction that relationship brings. The faculty governs many aspects of the law school, which means that at least a core group of the professors decides the policies of the school through debate and consensus. The kinds of policies for which the faculty is often responsible include employment, personnel, entry onto the faculty, admission to the law school, the curriculum of the law school, requirements for matriculation, and just about anything else that relates to how the law school functions. Because faculties must develop some level of relationship for this to work, joining a faculty is less like trying to get a job and more like trying to join a family. The unique nature of this workplace explains some of the quirks of the job and the hiring process. It also explains why the system has fostered so much homogeneity in law professors. Those with greater access to insiders in the system received the information contained in this book, while those with less access did not.

A NOTE ON TERMINOLOGY

Doctrinal Faculty Versus Skills Faculty

If you talk to law faculty about their jobs, or talk to faculty candidates, you will hear some phrases that require some explanation up front. First, a distinction is often made between "doctrinal" faculty and "skills" faculty. Doctrinal faculty are those faculty who teach the bread-and-butter courses of the law school curriculum—torts, contracts, constitutional law, property, criminal law, and so on. "Doctrinal" simply refers to the fact that the vast majority of the classes they teach are introductory survey courses covering the court-made (or statutory, regulatory, and court-supplemented) body of law of a particular subject. Doctrinal faculty may teach small upper-level seminars that are specialized, covering a topic in greater depth than the entry-level survey course, or one that is not usually covered in doctrinal surveys at all. Doctrinal faculty are usually on a career path that will end in receiving tenure and, eventually, promotion to full professor (more on both shortly).[4] Some doctrinal faculty, however, are not full-time doctrinal teachers and, thus, not on a tenure track. In many law schools, adjunct professors will teach doctrinal courses (often very early in the morning, very late in the afternoon, or in the evening).

Doctrinal faculty are contrasted with "skills" faculty. Skills faculty usually include legal writing professors and those who teach in a law school's legal clinic. Instead of teaching entry-level courses on substantive law, these professors will teach a particular aspect of lawyering that often transcends doctrinal

---

4. Doctrinal faculty, however, do not necessarily focus their research and writing on "doctrine," as discussed above. As we will see later, part of the institutional schizophrenia affecting law schools is that while much of the faculty work on cutting-edge empirical or theoretical or policy matters, most students still go to law school to get taught the doctrine and the legal thinking skills that they will use as practicing lawyers. Hence, at many law schools curricular needs sometimes exert a pull on hiring as faculty or deans argue that certain courses need coverage.

boundaries to more closely imitate various kinds of law practice, aspects like legal writing or trial practice. Those professors may supervise law students who receive a special state license to represent clients in legal disputes handled by the law school's clinic. While skills faculty may teach doctrinal classes, such classes are not the focus of their energies. Similarly, skills faculty are less likely to be on a tenure track, working instead on contracts renewed at various intervals after a performance review, which are intended as a tenure substitute.

In this chapter, and throughout the book, we will talk about legal writing and clinical faculty separately, but will use the term doctrinal faculty to describe the teaching position most candidates at the Faculty Recruitment Conference seek. Further, we want to make clear that we use these terms in a descriptive sense only—there are tensions on some faculties between doctrinal and skills faculty; in using the terms as we do in this chapter, we do not mean to enlist on either side of those controversies. Throughout this book we will tend to focus on the experience of the doctrinal professor. Where appropriate, however, we will comment on the experience of nondoctrinal faculty, especially where there is contrast between their experience and that of doctrinal faculty members.

Tenure-Track Versus Nontenure-Track Faculty

"Tenure" (and not, as Denning once thought, "ten-year") is in essence a guarantee of lifetime employment. Once granted to an academic, it means that person may be dismissed only for the gravest of infractions or in times of extraordinary financial exigency (and sometimes not even then). Tenure of academics is thought to confer independence and freedom to pursue lines of academic inquiry free from outside pressure. It is thought to be an essential aid to academic truth. For its detractors, tenure raises costs to entry for new hires, discourages innovation, removes accountability, and does so in exchange for very little.[5] Whatever one's views of tenure, it is the goal of every academic who has the opportunity to obtain it.

Most entry-level doctrinal positions are "tenure track" positions. This means that after a probationary period of anywhere from four to six years,[6] an entry-level professor (usually called an "assistant professor" or an "associate professor") will be evaluated by a committee of his or her tenured colleagues and a vote will be taken whether to recommend the candidate for tenure. The vote is based on effectiveness in teaching, scholarship, and service. The tenure applicant usually prepares a massive dossier that includes a formal application, articles, evaluations, and other materials for the committee. Committee

---

5. Many law schools (and some universities) are attempting to remedy this by requiring professors to fill out annual reports of their activities for the year. One usually has to meet with the dean after filing the report, and things like raises, leaves, and preference in scheduling classes can depend on how productive one has been over the past year. But you needn't worry about that at this point, because you haven't even been hired yet!

6. At most schools an untenured professor *must* go up for tenure in the fifth or sixth year.

members will often review student evaluations, evaluate classes they observe, and send scholarship out to external reviewers for comments. In some cases, the committee's recommendation is then forwarded to the faculty for a vote. Usually this vote is taken of the current tenured faculty only. In some cases a supermajority is required to vote tenure for the candidate. The faculty's vote is then forwarded to the dean. At other schools, the committee's recommendation goes only to the dean, and the rest of the faculty do not weigh in.

The dean will then usually adopt the committee's or the faculty's recommendation and forward it (if the law school is part of a university) to the appropriate committee of the parent university, where it goes to the president and, usually, the board of trustees for final approval. (There are as many forms of governance in law schools and universities as there are, well, law schools and universities, so the foregoing is a very general description of what can be an extremely bureaucratized process. As they say, your mileage may vary.)

At some schools tenure is accompanied by a promotion from assistant to associate professor. In some schools, however, the promotion from assistant to associate comes as part of a pretenure review; tenure is granted separately so one would progress from being an associate professor without tenure to one with tenure. A few schools grant full professor status upon receiving tenure. Sometimes promotion is accompanied by a raise in salary, sometimes not. Again, schools differ, and law schools' tenure policies differ a great deal from other academic disciplines, making it a topic to explore when interviewing with different schools.[7]

While most candidates who have met the law school's minimum requirements will receive tenure, those who do not must leave the law school. In most cases, the unsuccessful tenure candidate will be given a one-year contract during which time that professor must find another school, or leave teaching altogether. Failure to gain tenure is not necessarily a death sentence for a teaching career, but you will want to do everything in your power not to be in a position to test that.

Nontenure-track faculty do not have to worry about the stresses related to seeking tenure. Of course, their jobs are less secure as a result, and that imposes another, and simply different, form of pressure. The trend is toward a measure of job security after a probationary period that, while not providing as much security as tenure, could be its functional equivalent. Contracts may not be functionally equivalent, however, unless they are presumptively renewable. The structure of job security is quite different between clinical professors and legal writing professors, so we will discuss them separately.

Law schools began forming clinics in large numbers in the 1970s to provide students with real-world experience and to provide services to those

---

7. It can be a decade or more before an assistant professor of, say, history is eligible for tenure and many more years after that before he or she is eligible for full professorship. The timeline is much shorter in law schools. For a recent overview of tenure timelines at select law schools, see Duncan Hollis, *Tenure & Promotion Timelines: An International Track?*, OPINIO JURIS (Sept. 12, 2008), http://opiniojuris.org/2008/09/12/tenure-promotion-timelines-an-international-track/.

in the community who couldn't access legal help easily. By the early 1990s, nearly every law school in the country had a legal clinic, and clinical development further increased significantly with the release in 1992 of the MacCrate Report,[8] which called for an expansion of clinical training for law students.

Clinical professors have a form of job security that the accrediting body of the American Bar Association mandates. Clinical professors generally will be on their own tenure track, separate from that of the doctrinal faculty, or be on a contract system that mimics the tenure system: with a probationary period of short-term contracts followed by presumptively renewable long-term contracts of at least five years.[9] While clinical faculty are usually evaluated on the same criteria as doctrinal faculty—that is, teaching, scholarship, service—the expectations, especially for production of scholarship, are likely to be less than for doctrinal faculty, and some clinical jobs have no scholarship requirement at all.

The higher the "status" of the clinical job, the more likely it will be hired through the Association of American Law Schools (AALS) hiring conference in Washington, D.C. So, if a clinical position is tenured or tenure track like a doctrinal position, it is very likely the school will interview for that position at the conference. If the position is a short-term position like a fellowship program, or a temporary job paid for by grant money, applicants will apply directly to the school. There is no central place to find out about these openings, and some schools will hire informally from their own grads, or local lawyers they know in the community. The best way to find out about them is to ask an existing clinical professor to keep track of job announcements for you.

Legal writing professors do not have quite the same history. Legal writing was not treated as a specialty, nor were significant law school resources devoted to it at most schools, until the MacCrate Report criticized the writing deficiencies of graduating students and, in 1996, the American Bar Association (ABA) added an accreditation standard requiring each law school to offer "a program designed to provide its graduates with basic competence in legal analysis and reasoning, legal research, problem solving and oral and written communication."

Since 1996, many schools have professionalized the legal writing curriculum and broadened it significantly. The treatment of those professors, however, has not been uniform. Only about one quarter of legal writing professors are treated like clinical professors,[10] that is, put on their own tenure track or

---

8. In 1992, the American Bar Association Section of Legal Education and Admissions to the Bar, which is the body that accredits most law schools, issued a report prepared by a task force on law schools and the profession. The chair of that task force was Robert MacCrate, which is why the report bears his name.

9. SECTION OF LEGAL EDUC. & ADMISSIONS TO THE BAR, AM. BAR ASS'N, STANDARDS: RULES OF PROCEDURE FOR APPROVAL OF LAW SCHOOLS 40–41 (2005–2006) (Standard 405(c) & Interpretation 405-6).

10. For a summary of how some schools have done this and the implications of treating legal writing faculty like clinical faculty, see Melissa H. Weresh, *Form and Substance: Standards for Promotion and Retention of Legal Writing Faculty on Clinical Tenure Track*, 37 GOLDEN GATE U.L. REV. 281 (2007). This article has a large appendix that reproduces the policies of several schools. *Id.* at 329–459.

given a tenurelike contract system.[11] A majority of legal writing professors are on shorter-term contracts that are not capped—they can keep getting renewed with no limit—but are not presumptively renewable. The average length of time spent by legal writing professors at a school is between three and four years. The ABA accrediting body requires only that legal writing professors be given as much security as will attract and retain faculty qualified to provide high-quality instruction in legal writing and will safeguard academic freedom.

A FIELD GUIDE TO LEGAL ACADEMICS

Having disposed of those preliminaries, let's look in more detail at the various habitués of the law school and the responsibilities of each. In addition to the doctrinal professor, the clinician, the legal writing professor, and the law librarian, we introduce here the various law school administrators.

The Doctrinal Professor (*Professaurus Rex,* sometimes divided into subspecies *Professaurus Theoreticus Rex* and *Professaurus Empiricus Rex*)

Doctrinal professors view themselves as at the top of the hierarchy. These are the coveted jobs in the law school. They usually pay the most money, hold out tenure for those who meet the minimum qualifications, and (according to legal writing professors, clinicians, and some administrators) do the least work of anyone at the law school. Doctrinal professors usually teach three or four courses per year[12] and must write regularly[13] in order to secure tenure (and after tenure, to ensure continued raises). In addition to the regular survey courses, the doctrinal professor often has the opportunity to teach limited-enrollment, specialized seminars that relate to the professor's scholarship. Doctrinal professors are usually eligible for summer stipends to assist their writing, as well as other support, like the ability to hire research assistants paid by the school. They are also full members of the faculty with the right to vote on all matters coming before it (except, usually, in the case of a tenure vote, if the faculty member is not yet tenured).

---

11. This and other information comes from the annual survey done by the Association of Legal Writing Directors (ALWD) and the Legal Writing Institute (LWI). The survey can be found on ALWD's Web site, http://www.alwd.org.

12. The standard load at law schools is four courses per year. Some schools—particularly those interested in creating incentives for the production of scholarship—are moving to a three-course load for "productive" scholars who agree to produce a certain number of law review articles per year.

13. "Regularly" means different things at different schools, but for a large number of schools it means a law review article every year or two.

The Clinician (*Professaurus Practicalis*)

Many law schools operate clinics that represent, usually, low income clients in civil or criminal matters, most commonly litigation, but increasingly in transactional business, too. The clinics are staffed by third-year students who are able to represent clients in many states through special law licenses. These students, in turn, are supervised by clinicians, licensed lawyers who aid the students in the representation of the clinic's clients and who may teach special courses designed to prepare students for the clinic experience or doctrinal classes related to the types of cases the clinic handles. The clinical job, then, is a hybrid of teaching and practice. The clinical professor represents clients like any lawyer, but also teaches students how to represent clients, and mentors them in ways most practitioners (and doctrinal professors) cannot.

Clinical professorships may or may not be tenure track as described above. Even in places where the clinical professors are not tenure track, there may be a "Director" of the clinic (or clinics) who will likely be on a tenure track. Similarly, the requirements for scholarship may differ for clinicians. Requirements may range from no expectation of scholarship to an expectation that *some* scholarship (written for other clinicians about matters related to law school clinics or in the doctrinal area of the clinic's work) will be produced. At some schools, expectations for clinicians are no different than those for doctrinal faculty. Interestingly, while clinical positions are not possessed of the same prestige as doctrinal positions, students often think *more* of those professors supervising them in clinic than they do of their doctrinal professors. This often proceeds from a perception that the clinical professors, being actual practitioners, operate in the "real world," as opposed to doctrinal professors, about whom students sometimes harbor suspicions that they couldn't "make it" in practice.

Legal Writing Professors (*Professaurus Hardworkandnorespectus*)

As the name suggests, these professors teach first-year law students legal analysis, research, and communication in a way that bridges doctrinal subjects. Legal writing professors are charged with equipping law students with the tools that will be essential to their success in the profession, including synthesis of rules and legal reasoning. It is one of the most demanding jobs in the law school; one that requires skill, creativity, and the ability to communicate clearly. It is a difficult thing to get high-achieving students to critique their own thought process and writing. They have a difficult time evaluating an argument. They also resist the notion that there is anything in their writing to improve and often do not see the connection between writing and thinking. Further, some don't believe that a "mere" legal writing teacher could help them do so. Students (encouraged by upper-level students and by the mismatch between the amount of work and credit awarded for legal writing classes) tend to regard legal writing as a course in busywork and legal writing professors as demi-professors, not to be taken seriously. Some of this hostility is generated (or at least compounded) by the fact that students usually receive their first grades in legal writing classes. Ninety percent of the first-year students begin to realize that they might not be in the top 10 percent of their class. The lot of legal writing professors is made even harder by the low regard in which their doctrinal colleagues sometimes hold them.

At the same time, the close one-on-one work with students can be extremely rewarding in a way that cannot be duplicated in doctrinal classes. Legal writing professors are the ones who get to see first-year students try out being lawyers for the first time. They see that light bulb go on when students understand the process of legal reasoning or the way to make an argument. They also get to see students take risks and master skills that attorneys use every day. Legal writing professors see the direct effects of their teaching, and can see the product of their work, in a way doctrinal professors very rarely see.

Law Librarians (*Professaurus Shhhshhush*)

The ABA and AALS accreditation requirements have ensured that law libraries account for large portions of law schools' budgets. In addition to the cost of physical plant and collections, law libraries require staff to run them. According to the American Association of Law Libraries, academic law librarians serve the following roles: educating students and faculty about print and electronic resources available at the library and training them in the use of those resources; providing research assistance to students and faculty; making acquisitions for the library; and managing new materials and technology once acquired.[14] In some cases, the librarians work with legal writing professors, teaching students legal research to 1Ls and to upper-level students.

While most law librarians will have a masters of library science degree (MLS), a 1996 survey indicated that less than 30 percent had a J.D. as well, though that number includes librarians in all law libraries, not just those in law schools. According to one source, "Many academic law libraries require law degrees for reference librarians and many middle management positions. Since academic law library directors are usually members of the law school faculty, almost all of them will have law degrees."[15]

If you are interested in being a law librarian, you should seek out those who are currently serving as law librarians and ask them about their jobs. Information about accredited MLS programs is available on the American Library Association's Web site (www.ala.org), and the American Association of Law Libraries' Web site (www.aall.org) also contains a wealth of information.

---

14. *The Role of Academic Law Librarians*, in FINDING YOUR WAY IN THE INFORMATION AGE: THE MANY ROLES OF LAW LIBRARIANS, http://www.aall.org. For a useful—though now dated—snapshot of law librarians' duties, see Frank G. Houdek, compiler, "*A Day in My Law Library Life*," Circa 1997, 89 L. LIB. J. 157 (1997).

15. Mary Whisner, *Choosing Law Librarianship: Thoughts for People Contemplating a Career Move*, LLRX.COM (Aug. 2, 1999), http://www.llrx.com/node/19/print.

Law School Administrators (*Professaurus Bureaucraticus*)

Law school administrators are responsible for the day-to-day management of the law school. Most law schools have subdivided the job among the dean and one or more associate or assistant deans. The dean is like the managing partner at a law firm—some would say the world's most dysfunctional law firm, depending on the law school—with the faculty playing the role of the firm partners. The dean is charged with articulating and pursuing a vision for the law school and raising money to support its activities. Many law schools will also have an associate dean for academic affairs, which, to continue the law firm analogy, roughly corresponds to a law firm's professional personnel partner. The associate dean makes the schedule, supervises adjunct professors, handles grading matters, and, perhaps, student discipline. Finally, a number of law schools also have a dean akin to a firm's chief financial officer. This associate dean will work with the dean to budget, liaise with the university (unless the law school is stand-alone), and possibly assist with fundraising.

Depending on the size of the law school, additional deanships may be present. Admissions-director positions are becoming decanalized; a good number of law schools are also creating deans for student affairs and for faculty scholarship. With a few exceptions (deans of admissions, for example, may not even be lawyers), administrators will be tenured law school faculty who may even teach a class or two during the year. (Many deans like to teach at least one class to keep their hand in.) Unlike doctrinal faculty who generally are not required to remain at the law school during the summer, deans are often expected to be on-site twelve months out of the year; but, as mentioned, they have lighter class loads and are not expected to produce scholarship as regularly as full-time faculty members, if they are expected to produce at all.

Other Faculty You Might Encounter

Most law schools employ *adjunct professors*, full-time practicing lawyers who agree to teach a course on an as-needed basis. Adjuncts are not tenure track, do not attend faculty meetings, and usually have little contact with other faculty members. Schools often employ adjuncts to teach classes where practitioners who have day-to-day exposure to a subject area have a comparative advantage over doctrinal faculty who no longer practice law to any appreciable degree. In other cases, adjuncts may be used to provide coverage in a "hot" area in which there are no current faculty members with appropriate expertise or interest. Schools tend to use adjuncts to cover upper-level electives, as opposed to using them on first- or second-year required courses. Schools love adjuncts in part because they offer course coverage at a discount: Schools may pay them as little as $2,000 a course.

If more than one class in an area needs covering, or if schools find themselves needing to cover "core" courses, the dean will often try to find a *visiting professor* to substitute for shortages in course coverage caused by an unfilled vacancy on the faculty or by increased demand in a particular area. Visits are usually either denominated *look-see* visits, in which the visitor is being actively considered for a permanent place on the faculty, or *podium-fill* visits, which carry no expectation of consideration for any present or future vacancy. Some law schools with fairly broad summer course offerings use visiting professors in place of their own faculty, who often prefer to spend their summers writing or traveling.

ACADEMIA EST OMNIS DIVISA IN PARTES TRES: TEACHING, SCHOLARSHIP, SERVICE

Teaching

There is often tremendous focus placed on the production of scholarship in the legal academy. Job candidates ask about support for scholarship; in turn, they are often questioned closely about their scholarly agenda, and their candidacies can stand or fall on the basis of their "job talk" when interviewing at a law school. While we do not suggest that this focus is misplaced, we would observe that many candidates end up giving little thought to what we found to be the toughest part of the job, at least initially: teaching.

Since there is no real apprenticeship for would-be law professors the way there can be in Ph.D. programs, many professors end up simply trying to replicate the way they were taught in law school—in some cases using the same casebook and even the same classroom notes—in their own courses. Law students aren't the only ones who have difficulty analyzing their thought processes or understanding the learning process. Even though most schools now regularly "light-load" new professors in their first semester, first-time teachers often vastly underestimate the amount of time necessary to devote to that *one* course. An additional shock often occurs as grades from the first set of exams are turned in and the realization dawns that *two additional* class preparations are in the offing for the new semester!

This is not intended to be a primer on law school teaching; books and articles have already been written on the subject. And later, in chapter 7, we will suggest some steps that newly hired professors ought to take well before actually appearing on campus to reduce or ameliorate the anxieties of the first year. Here we simply want to describe what teaching actually *is*, and what it is not.

If you are like us, one of the biggest adjustments to law school was to its pedagogical style. No longer was the professor simply providing a body of information to be digested and regurgitated, as in undergraduate classes; now students were expected to take a hand in their education (and, if called upon, the education of others in the class). Sometimes it seemed that the whole point of law school classes was to unsettle whatever sense of "learning" one had achieved by reading and digesting the assignment. From a student's perspective, this looks even easier than having to prepare lectures—all you have to do is ask a couple of questions and respond to student answers with "Why?" or move to another hapless student and ask "What do you think about Ms. Jones' answer?" As you might guess, there is much more to law school teaching than asking unanswerable questions. In fact, you will soon discover that preparing lectures to deliver to students is *much* easier than conducting a good interactive class.

Teaching in law school often involves a delicate balance between covering a given amount of information that you feel all students leaving your class should be exposed to and trying to develop students' critical thinking skills. Much of the point of the "Socratic method," allegedly, is to do the latter; some professors view this as the end of legal pedagogy and would leave the former to bar review classes. Good professors approach their classes with an appreciation of what material in a given class lends itself to skill development, what is amenable to more active learning strategies, and what might best be delivered through a lecture. Good teachers accurately gauge the skill level of their classes, moving quickly enough to get through the syllabus and to keep the better students engaged, without ignoring or losing those in the middle and at the bottom. In many cases, it will take two or three years to get a feel for the material and for the type of classes that one has.

Teaching doctrinal classes also requires discerning judgment regarding which items to include and which to excise. Many classes that were formerly six-hour, two-semester classes have been reduced to four hours, as law schools move to reduce the number of courses students are required to take. This, too, requires both good judgment and a willingness to experiment. Your choice of coverage may not stay constant over the years, especially if you change casebooks from time to time.

All the difficulties described above are often magnified for "skills professors," like those teaching legal writing and legal research. It is amazing how quickly students internalize the notion that they should not be required to do anything other than take one exam in each of their courses at the end of the semester! Students will often regard frequent assignments and preexam evaluations as an extreme imposition and as so much busywork with little "real world" value. It is no surprise that legal writing and law library journals are often filled with interesting and innovative ideas for livening up subjects to promote student engagement.

Micro-choices accompany the macro matters described above. The first few times through, you will spend inordinate amounts of time preparing for class. New professors report spending upward of ten to fifteen hours or more for each class. That will quickly diminish over time, but intense time preparation as you prepare to face each day's classes is a fact of life for the first few years. All told, actual in-class time will pale in the first few years with the amount of out-of-class preparation for those fifty minutes.

Then there are matters as mundane as whether you will take roll (at schools where there is no formal attendance policy), whether or how you will call on students, whether you'll address them by first name or Mr. or Ms., how to handle students who are unprepared, whether to use assigned seating and a seating chart, and whether to set out the entire semester in the syllabus, for example. Even "experienced" teachers tend to be inveterate tinkerers, constantly revising syllabi, experimenting with teaching techniques, and contemplating various exercises to engage students. It does get easier over time, but teaching is always more time intensive than you expect.

Unfortunately, for the new professor, the end of the semester brings no relief. Aside from the very first few classes, nothing else triggers neophyte anxieties quite like writing and grading exams. Each set of exams, particularly the first, brings on new choices regarding coverage, difficulty level, style of exam, and method of grading. Exam-writing anxiety often sets in about halfway through the term, and is exacerbated by the common experience of the new professor managing to have forgotten by the tenth week what he or she taught in the third week. Moreover, you cannot just write the questions; it takes writing the answers as well to "debug" the questions. Are the questions too hard, in which case all you will get back is unfathomable glop? Are the questions too easy, in which case you will be unable to distinguish among them sufficiently to meet the school's requirement that X percent of the grades be at the bottom end of the curve?

Grading, too, will consume a good part of the winter and summer "vacations" that are the envy of our counterparts in practice. One quickly learns the truth of the cliché that law professors "teach for free" and "get paid for grading exams." Then there is the grading itself, during which first-time teachers often go through a series of emotions not unlike Kübler-Ross's five stages of grief. The first stage is realizing that not a single exam answer bears any relationship whatsoever to your model. The second stage is coming to understand that grading essays is either objectively subjective, or subjectively objective, or, in other words, that no "point" system on essay answers ever really works perfectly. The third stage sets in about halfway through the grading when the professor wonders if there has been any real principle involved in distinguishing one answer from another. And so on.[16]

A common misperception among lawyers who think about teaching is that it is something one could jump into "when I decide to retire" or that it is something one would be good at because "I love teaching continuing education courses." In truth, the first few years of teaching would be as demanding and time-consuming as private practice *even if that were the only responsibility of the new professor.* As we shall see in the remainder of this chapter, teaching may be important, it may even be the most time consuming initially, but it is certainly not the *only* part of the job that claims a professor's time.

---

16. This description is perhaps unduly downbeat. One comes to the realization fairly quickly that there is a certain amount of arbitrariness in small differences, and there will be some inevitable inequities, say at the margin between a B+ and a B, or worse, between an A− and a B+. But the reality is that most professors come to find that conscientious and fair grading usually distinguishes As, Bs, and Cs fairly well, at least in broad strokes. And there is no sense of relief like filling the grades into the final grading report for submission to the registrar. It's also an interesting experience to get back the key that links blind grading exam numbers to students, particularly in the first year, when you try to recall who that student was who never said a word the entire semester, but got the highest grade in the class.

Scholarship

There was a time in the academy in which new faculty were hired with no expectation of prior publications and were expected to turn out a small number (two, sometimes fewer) articles prior to receiving tenure, with no expectation of regular publication thereafter. Those days are gone, even in schools occupying the lower tiers of the *U.S. News & World Report* survey. In fact, a common refrain heard from older members of appointments committees and in faculty hiring meetings is that "well, *I* could have never gotten hired today."

The production of scholarship is now a large part of the doctrinal professor's life at most law schools. Many entry-level candidates will now have—indeed, should have—at least one law review publication, and may have more than one. (Appendix B, at the end of this book, contains a brief primer on law review submissions.) We say "should have" because once on the faculty, untenured professors are generally expected to produce at least three major articles in five years before being considered for tenure. Only by actually doing legal scholarship will you know whether that prospect is exciting or excruciating to contemplate. The articles are expected to make some contribution to the field, as opposed to just summarizing judicial doctrine in a particular area or giving an overview of an area of the law. At some schools, the articles have to be of a certain page length, with requirements about the "quality" of placement. For example, a school might require that the articles be between forty and sixty pages and be published in law reviews of ABA-accredited schools of reputation equal to the law school's own law review. At many schools, the publication requirement is even more rigorous. These articles will then be evaluated by professors at other schools at the time the professor goes up for tenure. Clinical, legal writing, and law librarian faculty—especially those who are on a tenure track—will be expected to write as well. Some will choose to write in traditional doctrinal areas, but some significant portion focus their writing in their particular skill areas.[17]

As mentioned above, many schools are creating decanal positions responsible for encouraging the production and dissemination of faculty scholarship. New faculty scholarship is often a particular focus of scholarship deans. This combination of trends means that "early and often" is the new mantra for faculty scholarship. Scholarship thus represents another significant draw on the time of all faculty—particularly new hires and the untenured. Even if you are one of the lucky souls for whom ideas flow freely and writing is nearly effortless, you have not been hired solely for your scholarly prowess. Thus, scholarship becomes merely one of those insistent creditors to whom you owe time.

---

17. Or they should, at any rate. It is not uncommon to hear of doctrinal faculty denigrating nondoctrinal scholarship because it isn't, well, doctrinal scholarship. It would be important for candidates in these fields not only to understand what the paper requirements are, but also how those requirements are applied in practice. This is not to say, of course, that nondoctrinal faculty don't produce excellent doctrinal scholarship as well.

Moreover, it is here that procrastination and lassitude pose severe hazards for those who are not self-starters. Sooner or later, if your classes are a disaster (or if you are not showing up for them at all), the assistant dean and several of your experienced colleagues will likely intervene. By contrast, you can put off writing for any number of good reasons (the pressures of teaching, of family, of responsibilities at the law school, etc.) until the very eve of tenure, at which point it will likely be too late. Schools often try to minimize this possibility by having some sort of pretenure review; and scholarship deans are supposed to watch for problems with new faculty. The fact remains, however, that no one but you can write your articles. All the assistance and support in the world cannot sit you in a chair and release you only after you've written 1,000 words for the day. And if you do not have a passionate sense that you have something (several things, in fact) important to say and that you will not be content until you say them in print, writing law review articles will be agony.

We should add a few words to reiterate an earlier point about what it means to do doctrinal scholarship, and this may vary from school to school. A practicing lawyer, whether relatively new or well-seasoned, may have ruminated about that knotty little problem in mens rea, the rule in Shelley's case, the dead man's statute, the business judgment rule, promissory estoppel, or something like that. For the last twenty-five years or so, legal scholarship, particularly in law schools that are part of research universities, has moved to "law and [something]." The great advantage of having some practice experience is that you have rich soil from which theoretical ideas may sprout. But if you stick to the language of practice, and never move into the other circle of theory, you will not be effective in persuading an appointments committee that you are ever going to deserve to be a tenure-track faculty member. Indeed, if you never look at a piece of your own writing and wonder if you are not really arguing about the number of angels dancing on the head of a pin, it's likely you are not getting close enough to the theoretical line.

A long-time tax practitioner with a substantial publication record, including some law reviews, approached one of us for advice in approaching the law school hiring process. This is what we said:

> Mere volume of writing may not establish academic chops, even if published in general law reviews, if the writing has only been practitioner-oriented.

> The real trick is establishing a unique viewpoint. Is there a theme that runs through your work on which you can give a three-minute summary to a faculty appointments committee of nontax people? There is going to be a question at some point in the hiring process that is the sine qua non of your entry into academia after all those years of practice that goes something like this: "So, what is it about your scholarship and writing that is fresh and exciting, will draw attention to you, and in the process, distinguish our faculty and our school?" And the answer must be meaningful in the academic, not just the practice, sense.

> It seems like the vast majority of young law professors want to talk and write about the burning constitutional, political, and rights issues of the

day. It's an advantage to want to teach and write in a niche that may be considered more mundane (somebody has to think about employee benefits, for example). But merely writing in the niche is not enough; you need to have something scholarly to say about it.

Service

The final component of academia is usually overlooked, but its demands can overwhelm those of either teaching or scholarship. "Service" consists of formal service on university or law school committees, such as the hiring and tenure, admissions, appointments, curriculum, or academic standards committees. Coaching moot court teams, advising student organizations, participating in alumni functions, organizing symposia, and teaching continuing legal education (CLE) courses are other forms that service might take. But service will also involve any number of informal duties that one takes on for the good of the law school. Having dinner with faculty candidates, interviewing scholarship applicants, hosting prospective students, judging practice moot court rounds, attending student orientation, and greeting law school visitors are just a few other things that are often part of every law professor's life. Service may also encompass service to the local or national bar, service to the local community, or even acting as counsel in a public interest or pro bono case.

Expanding the definition in this way, though, does not quite capture the term's range. Particularly with new professors (often younger and perceived as more approachable), students will begin clamoring for your attention, seeking advice on a bewildering array of professional and personal matters. Students will request that you write recommendations for them to employers, judges, and state bar examiners. Some will seek constant reassurance that they are "getting it." Others will just decide that they like you and will not have any compunction about stopping by because they were ready to take a study break. Female and minority professors (particularly on faculties with few of either) can find themselves overwhelmed with these informal service duties. And legal writing and clinical professors, because of their closer contact with students, tend to be called on as well.

The good news is that new professors will usually be spared onerous committee work for the first year or two. The bad news is that noncommittee service, as well as the informal mentoring, will start as soon as you step on campus. Often the law school will want to showcase the new talent to prospective students and alumni; students will regard younger professors as approachable and presume you to be sympathetic. This fact means that you must be an effective time manager, self-aware enough to know when you have too much on your plate, and confident enough to say no when you are getting too swamped. A hallmark of overwork is when, however much you enjoy it, these demands on your time are detracting from class preparation, your writing time, or both.

SO YOU THINK YOU CAN TEACH?

If you have made it this far in the book, we hope that we have complicated your view of law professors a bit. We hope it's clear that there is often much more to teaching in a law school than most students (and lawyers) perceive. We also hope we have highlighted the different jobs that coexist on a law school faculty. We have also tried to illuminate some of the aspects of the job that make it a challenging one that, however attractive it might seem from the outside, is not for everyone. At this point it is worth asking yourself whether, based on what you know, you want to go to the time and expense (including actual and opportunity costs) to attempt to secure a position on a law school faculty. A further question might be what *kind* of law teaching job appeals to you.

At a minimum, we think that successful candidates ought to be able to demonstrate to potential employers they possess the following traits:

> *Intellectual curiosity.* This is essential. If you are not excited about the subjects you will be teaching, you cannot expect students to be. And you cannot effectively help students with the material without being willing to engage it from different perspectives yourself. Moreover, you will never produce any scholarship worthy of the name in a subject in which you have no real interest. Finally, most of your colleagues won't be doing work in your area, but you will be attending dozens of formal and informal faculty colloquia. Success in the academy doesn't necessarily turn on engaging with colleagues' ideas, but an eagerness to do so can't hurt and will make the whole experience a lot more pleasant.

> *Being a self-starter.* Even as a new professor you will be largely unsupervised. It is up to you to prepare for class, grade and return assignments, and tend to your scholarship. You will usually receive whatever help you need simply by asking, but there are several things (teaching your classes, writing your articles, grading your exams) that only you can do. You should be honest with yourself whether this is a trait you possess.

> *Patience.* This is an indispensable trait that you will need to have not only with your students but with yourself and your colleagues as well. Your law students are likely to present themselves at all ability levels. Even if material seems crystal clear to you, you will have to tolerate even the most basic questions with aplomb, or risk discouraging that student from ever asking a question or coming to see you during office hours again. It helps to realize, at some level, how much you have learned and how far you have come since you were in your students' shoes. The days of the Kingsfield-like tyrant are gone; no one thinks that ridicule, sarcasm, humiliation, and condescension are effective teaching techniques. If you doubt this, listen to Pink Floyd's "Another Brick in the Wall" again. ("No dark sarcasm in the classroom/Teacher leave them kids alone.") Patience with self is equally as important. Your first classes are going to be like

first drafts of articles—rough. If you place unrealistic expectations on yourself in your teaching and your scholarship, you will wreck your health and probably not improve much either. This patience requires a long view, as well. Every time you begin a semester, you start over from scratch with a new group of students and you'll have to think of yet more ways to come at the same problems. Such Sisyphean labor can either be very demoralizing or (as we see it) an exciting challenge. Finally, you need patience when dealing with your colleagues. You may have distinct ideas about how your law school ought to run. They may be fabulous ideas. Not surprisingly, your colleagues may have different ideas. Even if they agree with you, change at schools can be glacial. Nowhere is patience more of a virtue than on a faculty. If you insist that everyone who disagrees with your ideas—ideas that to you are self-evidently correct—is a fool or a knave, you'll be eating lunch alone a lot and will ensure your good ideas are always disregarded.

> *Confidence that stops short of arrogance.* Let's face it, standing in front of a class every day and "professing" requires self-confidence. You will make mistakes, students will ask you questions you can't answer, and occasionally you'll have a bad class. Those things make teaching humbling as well, especially at first. But you have to accept them as part of the job and not allow them to paralyze you. At the same time you cannot, because of your position, pretend infallibility. Confidence married with a healthy self-deprecation is essential to get through the first few classes, especially if you're teaching a class you've never taught before. A certain self-awareness is also helpful; you should be your toughest critic, but you should also accept the feedback you get from students and from colleagues as offering some value. Even if you disagree with the substance of that feedback, it gives you the opportunity to reflect on your work. This is not a job that provides the kinds of positive feedback that you might get working for someone else, nor the court victories if you were a litigator. You have to have enough confidence not to need that external validation on any sort of regular basis.

> *Perseverance.* Related to both patience and confidence is perseverance, both in the job search and upon entry into the academy. Rejection is far more common than acceptance, whether it be in article submission or job application. Compared to what you may have experienced in school or in law practice, you are judged in the academy by a wide range of people, whether they be five to ten member appointments committees who interview you, fifteen to sixty member faculties who listen to your job talk, the 150 people who download your article from SSRN, the hundreds of people who read a blog post, or the dozens of students whom you teach. In all of those people, in all of those audiences, somebody is almost certain not to like you or your work! So you can't get discouraged too easily when things don't go well or as planned; it will be difficult to do your job if you do. You cannot stop showing up for your classes because of a couple of unsuccessful ones. You can't stop writing because your first article—the one you naturally consider to be brilliant—wasn't accepted

by the *Harvard Law Review*, and was, in fact, rejected by any number of lesser journals. Networking is important both during the job search and upon appointment. Seek out friends and correspondents as you begin to think about your scholarly ideas, and even before you start in on the actual application process. If you land at a school with a close-knit faculty where your colleagues are around and able to buck up your spirits, this will be easier. But you may just as easily get a job at a large law school where faculty come in (sometimes at different times of the day), teach, meet, but do much of their work from home. At such schools you might have to work harder to find mentors, connect with colleagues, and develop other sources of aid or inspiration.

> *Collegiality.* Teaching and writing can be solitary endeavors. At the same time, you must not lose sight of the fact that you are part of a community made up of students, faculty, staff, and university colleagues, as well as other scholars in your field. You will have to interact with all groups on a regular basis. If you really don't like people, then this is probably not the job for you. The academy may be something of a refuge from the work-a-day world, but it is most certainly not a cloister.

> *Willingness to accept a pay cut.* Compared to other academics, law professors—particularly doctrinal professors—do well. Relative to partners in law firms, however, law professors' salaries tend to plateau early and stay flat (rising slightly with the cost of living, supplemented perhaps by merit raises for productive faculty) for the remainder of one's career. With rare exceptions, there aren't many opportunities to make outside income—contrary to the beliefs of many law students that their professors are able to print money by consulting. Confronting the pay-cut question is especially important if your successful candidacy will uproot your family. There are upsides to the legal academic life, but—though the folks in the English Department won't believe it—remuneration isn't one of them.

Another important consideration is what type of law professor you want to be. Again, the answer to this question will depend heavily on what you want out of the position, and where your strengths lie. If prestige and salary are important to you, then you will likely be unhappy as a clinician or a legal writing professor. Conversely, if you cannot imagine anything worse than having to write a long, heavily footnoted article at least once every year or so, then being a doctrinal professor might seem less like a dream job and more like indentured servitude.

One way to get answers to some of these questions is to talk to law professors you know—friends, mentors, old professors, friends of friends. You'll need to reestablish contact with them at some point anyway if you go forward, so the earlier the better. Tell them that you are investigating the possibility of being a teaching candidate and ask them what they like and don't like about their jobs. Ask them what they do on an average day: how much time is taken up preparing for class, meeting with students, doing committee work. Ask them when they write, if they write. Ask them to introduce you to others, especially recent hires, and contrast their answers with those of more established professors.

One sure-fire way to experience the life of a law professor is to try it for a time, or as Professor Mike Madison has said, quoting Chevy Chase in *Caddyshack*: "Be the ball."[18] If you live in a city with a law school, inquire about adjunct opportunities to teach a doctrinal class or a legal writing class. Law schools often employ a number of adjuncts to teach sections of legal writing; they often prefer to have practitioners teach first-years who are working on appellate briefs. If you teach in an esoteric area—like tax, estates and trusts, environmental law, and the like—there may be even more opportunities. The pay will be modest, and if you're still in practice, it will eat up a chunk of your free time, but the experience will be invaluable, and will likely be a plus if you decide to become a candidate down the road. Be careful not to get so much experience as an adjunct that you don't have time to write.[19] Use this primarily as a way to test your interest in teaching.

The same goes for producing scholarship; you'll never know until you try. Start small; your first law review article will not likely make it into the *Harvard Law Review*. And if you're still practicing, writing during your spare time can be downright brutal—lots of late nights and weekend afternoons in the library or at your computer. Write a piece for your bar journal, or try to develop some CLE materials into a substantive, scholarly law review article.[20] There are excellent books to aid you in organizing and writing law review articles.[21] The key for your first article is to try to leverage intellectual capital you already possess. Try writing; see how you like it. Imagine being expected to do something like that as a regular part of your day. You should be able to tell relatively quickly whether it is something that excites and motivates you. If it is not, but you're still attracted to the idea of teaching students, perhaps you should consider skills positions like clinician or legal writing professor.

---

18. Mike Madison, *The Meat Market*, MADISONIAN (Oct. 26, 2004), http://madisonian .net/archives/2004/10/26/the-meat-market/.

19. Brad Wendel, *The Big Rock Candy Mountain: How to Get a Job in Law Teaching*, answer to Q: "I don't relish the thought of spending my time writing law review articles. Is there still a place in law teaching for me?," http://ww3.lawschool.cornell.edu/faculty-pages/ wendel/teaching.htm (last visited July 8, 2010).

20. To be clear, law reviews won't publish CLE materials, but the materials could serve as the basis for a substantive piece that they *would* publish.

21. *See* Eugene Volokh, *Academic Legal Writing: Law Review Articles, Student Notes, Seminar Papers, and Getting on Law Review* (3d ed. 2007); *see also* Elizabeth Fajans & Mary R. Falk, *Scholarly Writing for Students: Seminar Papers, Law Review Notes, and Law Review Competition Papers* (3d ed. 2005). Although these books are student resources, they also provide valuable information for scholars who are no longer students.

Where Do Law Professors Come From?

"Okay," you may be saying to yourself, "I now understand that there are differences among law professors and that different positions may each have a different focus. And I understand that law professors have a lot to do other than just teach a few hours a week." But, you might continue, "How did they get to where they are? Where *do* law professors come from? Do they share common characteristics? What do law schools look for in candidates?"

This chapter is intended to answer those questions, with a view to helping you choose among the various paths to the profession. As we have tried to make clear from the introduction, and this can't be emphasized enough: There really is no *easy* way. Some paths are, however, definitely easier than others and some would-be candidates have more to overcome initially before they even get *on* a path. Moreover, despite the different possible paths, successful candidates will tend to share common attributes.

In this chapter, we will indulge in a bit of oversimplified classification to make our point that some paths are easier than others, and that candidates ought to do everything they can to ensure their path is one of the easier ones. In the pages that follow, we will talk about the *Standard Model*, the *Revised Standard Model*, and the *Nonstandard Model* candidate.[1] Within each model, moreover, there are variations on the theme. While we do not claim that our classifications and subdivisions exhaust all possibilities, we are confident that they represent the backgrounds of the lion's share of successful candidates.

The second part of this chapter offers some advice on how to upgrade from a Nonstandard Model to a Revised Standard candidate. Three primary options are used to maximize a person's chances: publishing, getting a Master of Laws (LL.M.) from an elite law school, or pursuing a visiting assistant professorship or other fellowship position. Visiting assistant professorships (VAPs) and fellowships designed for those interested in teaching and publishing are on the rise. Specialized LL.M.s and Doctors of Juridical Science

---

1. Brian Leiter uses a similar taxonomy, but does not cover what we call the Nonstandard Model candidate. His categories are the Classical Path, the Modified Classical Path, and the Interdisciplinary Path. Brian Leiter, *Paths to Law Teaching* (Aug. 2009), http://www.law.uchicago.edu/careerservices/pathstolawteaching.

(S.J.D./J.S.D.), the terminal law graduate degree, are additional paths some pursue, but they may not offer as much of a competitive advantage to a candidate.

Finally, we discuss the importance of writing and publishing as part of becoming a viable candidate. This is important not only as a matter of differentiating yourself from other candidates and other LL.M., VAP, or fellowship applicants, but it serves as a proxy for ambition and ability to pursue a scholarly agenda.[2] Scholarly promise is important because that is, in part, what a school's *U.S. News & World Report* rankings are based on and it's what legitimizes law schools within the academy.[3] And so once hired, publishing is essential to getting tenure. In part, it is essential to tenure because tenure is easy to obtain in law schools, relative to many other disciplines. The bane of law schools is the tenured faculty member who stops publishing. A professor who is prolific pretenure is likely to continue to write posttenure as well. Likewise, a candidate who is prolific prehiring is unlikely to be a problem come tenure consideration. The bottom line is that you should write early and often. To that end, we offer some food for thought about preparing to do precandidacy research and writing.

We begin, however, with a more general discussion about all of the kinds of proxies that law schools often rely on to separate viable candidates from those they will not bother to interview.

WHAT DO LAW SCHOOLS WANT FROM CANDIDATES?

Candidates and Merit Badges

Law school appointments committees tend to be a pretty conservative lot. And their job is actually quite difficult. As Randy Barnett has said, "Put yourself in the position of an appointments committee member charged with filling 20 interview slots from the 700–900 one page resumes you leaf through. How do you choose?"[4] Members tend to favor candidates who possess several proxies for curiosity and intelligence thought to ensure future success as faculty members. Each qualification, or merit badge, as we call them,

> is an indication that other people have vetted the candidate already. After the law school admissions process vets you, there comes

---

2. Randy Barnett, *Getting a Law Teaching Job*, VOLOKH CONSPIRACY (Mar. 9, 2005, 6:09 PM), http://volokh.com/posts/chain_1110176668.shtml.

3. Brad Wendel, *The Big Rock Candy Mountain: How to Get a Job in Law Teaching*, answers to questions "What makes a candidate stand out?" and "What's wrong with publishing in bar journals? What's so great about law review articles? Do law schools just have a footnote fetish?," http://ww3.lawschool.cornell.edu/faculty-pages/wendel/teaching.htm (last visited July 8, 2010).

4. Barnett, *supra* note 2.

grades by each professor, law review competition (grades and, in some schools, writing), vetting by judges hiring clerks, vetting by law firms. The more competitive is each vetting and the more vettings a candidate passes, the more attractive he or she looks to a committee member with very limited information about each applicant.[5]

As Brad Wendel has added,

In an ideal world, appointments committees would not have to rely on proxies for the one thing they care most about—promise as a scholar . . . —and would somehow be able to measure it directly. But of course, there is no way to directly measure scholarly promise, so traditionally committees rely on pedigree . . . as an indirect measure.[6]

The following represent a partial list of these "merit badges":

> Ivy League (or Ivy-equivalent) J.D. or Ivy League LL.M.
> Prestigious fellowship or VAP
> Prior publications (either as a student or after graduation)
> High grades and honors as law student and as undergraduate
> Judicial clerkship experience (especially appellate court clerkships)
> Law review experience (especially editorial experience)
> Some (but not too much) practice experience

The weight given to each will vary depending upon the law school and upon each committee member's own view of what matters most. We know of highly credentialed candidates with a list of impressive writings who have not been given an interview because committee members of schools stressing professional training thought their backgrounds to be insufficiently practical.[7] On the other hand, given the importance that most law schools assign to the *U.S. News & World Report* rankings and the weight that survey puts on reputation of faculty, it is fair to say that it is becoming imperative for law schools at all levels to hire faculty who will be publishing quality legal scholarship at regular intervals. Thus, we think that the amount of writing that one has published *before* going on the market can operate as a powerful trump, compensating for the absence of one or more of the usual proxies. And we know several people currently teaching for whom this has seemed to be true.

As you will see in the pages that follow, the various candidacy models that we sketch here possess the merit badges listed above, some more than others and in greater quantities.

---

5. *Id.*

6. Wendel, *supra* note 3, answer after question "Why are law schools so fixated on prestige?"

7. For more about the different types of law schools one might encounter as a candidate, see chapter 4.

Models of Candidacy

The Standard Model (Elite and Super-Elite)

Like it or not, the data says that the most important aspect of the Standard Model candidate is having received a J.D. from an Ivy League or Ivy League-equivalent law school.[8] Standard Model Super-Elite candidates not only have such a degree, but held an editor position at the school's main law review, published a note or comment, and finished at or near the top of their class—assuming their law school still issues grades to students. Upon graduation, Standard Model Super-Elites clerked for a respected Court of Appeals judge (a lucky few will have clerked on the U.S. Supreme Court) and then joined a large law firm or worked in a prestigious law position for the federal government (e.g., the Office of Legal Counsel, the Solicitor General's office, the appellate division of the Department of Justice, the Office of Legal Advisor to the State Department) before becoming a candidate. If you are a Standard Model Super-Elite candidate, congratulations.

But even relatively few of those who went to elite schools have all of those merit badges. And some of our colleagues maintain that a true Standard Model Super-Elite candidate would also possess a Ph.D. in subjects like history, economics, political science, or philosophy. So although it might seem that they have the most important credential, an Ivy League J.D. or its equivalent, the reality for most Standard Model Elite candidates is that the process is still highly competitive, the likelihood of success is relatively low, and the other merit badge achievements are almost as important for them as for the Revised Standard and Nonstandard Models.

Having said that, if you happen to be reading this as an undergraduate and are interested in teaching at the law school level, *the Standard Model Elite, even if not Super-Elite, is the person you want to be when you graduate from law school.* Trust us, being the Standard Model Elite candidate makes going through the hiring process, while still stressful, less so than for those with degrees from non-elite schools. Likely your biggest concern will be fitting all of your interviews into two days.[9] If it's too late for you to be a Stan-

---

8. Brian Leiter's study of 730 law professors either tenured or on a tenure track in the 2001–2002 school year demonstrated that over one-third had earned a J.D. from Yale, Harvard, or Stanford. Brian Leiter, *Where Tenure Track Faculty Went to Law School, 2000–02*, BRIAN LEITER'S LAW SCHOOL RANKINGS, http://www.leiterrankings.com/faculty/2000faculty_education.shtml (last visited July 9, 2010). As noted in the introduction, Professor Lawrence Solum also does an annual entry-level hiring report on his Legal Theory Blog. His analysis of the 2008–2009 hiring season as of April 26, 2009, showed 150 new hires in total, of which 116 or over 76 percent were from the following schools: Yale, 26; Harvard, 26; Berkeley, 11; Michigan, 11; Stanford University, 10; Columbia, 10; NYU, 10; Chicago, 6; Georgetown University, 3; Minnesota, 3. The results of the 2009–2010 season were down in terms of absolute numbers of hires, but almost as skewed: of 101 reported hires, seventy (or just under 70 percent) were from the following schools: Yale, 18; Harvard, 17; NYU, 8; Columbia, 5; Virginia, 5; Berkeley, 4; Penn, 4; Stanford University, 3; Michigan, 3; Chicago, 3.

9. That's a reference to the two-day AALS Faculty Recruitment Conference, otherwise known as the "meat market," which we'll get to in chapter 3.

dard Model Elite candidate, read on! The good news is that the Standard Model Elite is not the only way to get hired at a law school.

In Memoriam: The Standard Model (Non-Elite Version)

It was not so long ago that a (or *the*) top graduate at non-elite law schools could have success on the academic job market. In all respects, the Standard Model Non-Elite candidate looked like the candidate described above, except he or she would *not* have an Ivy League J.D. and probably did not have as prestigious a clerkship. More likely the Standard Model Non-Elite candidate excelled at a state law school or regional private law school, clerked for a district judge or even the state supreme court, and may have earned his or her legal spurs at a regional, not a national, law firm. Aside from student work on the law review, the Standard Model Non-Elite candidate probably hadn't written anything. And yet, these candidates were often hired by non-elite law schools whose faculty saw their mission as training lawyers, not churning out reams of esoteric law review articles. Some of these schools would even hire their own top graduates after a decent interval in practice.

Alas, the hiring practices of most schools have changed sufficiently to make the Standard Model Non-Elite not so "standard" anymore. Indeed, we would consider such a candidate a Nonstandard Model candidate whose success on the market would be the exception rather than the rule. However, examples of this model still exist on law school faculties at many schools, are often heard to complain loudly about the seemingly endless procession of candidates with little or no practical experience, and chide their colleagues on the appointments committee for mindless credentialism in selecting candidates to interview.

The Revised Standard Model

So what hope is there for candidates who *didn't* go to that Ivy League school but did well in law school, have exhibited a potential for scholarship, and who, thirty-odd years ago, might have fit the Standard Model Non-Elite candidate described above? Fortunately, there is what we call a "Revised Standard Model" candidate. This candidate has done very well (top 10 percent or so) at a good state or private, non-Ivy law school, including service on the law review and a judicial clerkship, along with some practice experience at a highly regarded regional or national law firm. (This is where the primary advantage of being Standard Model Elite kicks in. It is relatively common that Standard Model Elite hirees, while having otherwise proved their academic bona fides, have not been members or editors of the main law review, and, while academically successful, not necessarily Order of the Coif or top ten percent.) Where the Revised Standard Model differs from the Standard Model Non-Elite is that the former will usually launder that non-elite law school degree at an Ivy League institution. Yale, Harvard, and Columbia have well-regarded LL.M. programs designed to burnish the credentials of law professor wannabes who weren't able to get their J.D.s at those institutions.

For the LL.M., you may also be able to substitute a prestigious fellowship—Harvard's Climenko Fellows or Chicago's Bigelow program are the paradigms—or a stint as a visiting assistant professor (VAP). Fellowships and VAPs have the advantage of offering the ability to get actual teaching experience (usually involving a legal writing class, but some offer the opportunity to teach a class of your choosing as well) with more time to write than you might otherwise have while taking a full load of classes. Furthermore, fellows and VAPs usually have the opportunity to participate in faculty workshops, which can be invaluable preparation for the "job talk" you will give when you are invited back to schools following the Association of American Law Schools (AALS) hiring meeting. What better way to figure out whether you like being a law professor or to internalize the norms of law faculty than to be one, even if only for a short-term appointment? (For more on both, see the discussion later in this chapter, and in chapter 8.)

Nonstandard Model(s)

But wait, there's more! It is possible to join the faculty of law schools *without* following the paths described above. Success from following nonstandard paths is rare, however. For example, it is possible, but difficult, to *trade up*—moving from a clinical or legal writing position to a doctrinal position. One could also *go for broke*—ignoring the claimed necessity of obtaining an LL.M. or a fellowship and simply filling out the form and going on the market. There are also a certain number of candidates for whom candidacy represents a significant career change: long-time practitioners, government officials, or even academics in other disciplines who have decided to capitalize on law schools' growing interest in interdisciplinary studies.

We know examples of current doctrinal faculty members who took each of those paths. But anyone contemplating becoming a Nonstandard Model candidate should be aware of significant obstacles that will have to be overcome. For the go-for-broke candidate, the obstacle will likely be the innate conservatism of law school hiring committees. Candidates who lack elite credentials, even if they have significant pluses, will often simply be overlooked by those who presume that a truly special candidate would have found some way to get elite validation of that fact. Call this the "if you're so smart, why didn't you go to Harvard or Yale" problem.

Candidates seeking to trade up will have to overcome another problem: the tendency of doctrinal faculty to be dismissive of clinicians and legal writing professors—especially those who aspire to doctrinal positions. This is the "if you're so smart, how come you're not already a *real* law professor" problem; and yes, we've actually heard the "real" law professor terminology thrown out in this context. Moreover, to the extent that the committee contains legal writing faculty or clinicians, those members might resent a candidate with that background who seeks a doctrinal position, viewing it as treasonous. This might be termed the "Do you think you're too smart to be a clinician/legal writing instructor?" problem. (If you find it difficult to believe that intelligent people would be so petty, it's probably a good time to introduce you to the catechism of the academy. Q: Why are faculty politics so brutal? A: Because the stakes are so low.)

Nonstandard Model candidates who seek academic jobs after long periods of private practice or government service will face a number of questions about capability and motivation.[10] Committee members will wonder whether the candidate plans to be a productive member of the faculty if hired, or simply views it as an opportunity to retire but still receive a generous salary. (Or worse, receive a generous salary in addition to running a solo practice on the side!) The fact that every year plenty of candidates with this outlook go through the process or contact schools outside of the process reinforces this fear.

Finally, "interdisciplinarity" is all the rage in law schools, and holding a Ph.D. in an area likely to enhance one's "law and" scholarship can aid a Nonstandard Model candidate. This comes (like most everything else) with a caveat. Candidates holding Ph.D.s can nevertheless encounter resistance from law school hiring committees, especially at non-elite law schools who view themselves as professional schools first and foremost. Incredibly, some law schools will consider candidates holding Ph.D.s "too academic" for the law school! Some faculty members are suspicious that the Ph.D. refugee doesn't *really* care about teaching bread-and-butter courses, but will demand esoteric seminars in what skeptics inevitably refer to as "Law and Basket Weaving"— although none of us is aware of graduate programs in basket weaving. At the extreme are those faculty who view any encroachment on the autonomy of the legal curriculum as unacceptable dilution of law's purity. There is a story from Denning's faculty about a former dean who said to one of his professors that the law school had "one of the best history departments in the state"; it was several years before the colleague to whom the remark was addressed realized that the dean *wasn't* being complimentary.

MAXIMIZING OPTIONS FOR THE NONSTANDARD CANDIDATE

What is a Nonstandard Model candidate to do? There are at least two possibilities for becoming a Revised Standard Model candidate that we will discuss here, because they represent the most promising methods of compensating for not having gone to an elite law school in the first place: publishing, and getting an elite LL.M., VAP, or fellowship. In fact, to maximize your chances on the hiring market, you ought to do more than one of these. Publishing will

---

10. Notwithstanding anything you have read to this point, long periods of private practice after the time Standard Model candidates generally go on the market converts a Standard Model Elite (or, we suspect, even a Standard Model Super-Elite) into a Nonstandard Model. Lipshaw falls into this category, having entered the academy on a normal tenure track after twenty-six years of practice in law firms and corporations, something that is very rare. For advice particular to the long-standing practitioner, see Jeffrey M. Lipshaw, *Memo to Lawyers: How Not to Retire and Teach*, 30 N.C. CENT. L. REV. 151 (2008).

increase your chances of being admitted to an elite LL.M. program (whose classes are often quite small, meaning that admission is usually very competitive) or obtaining a VAP or fellowship. Publishing early and often will also send signals that you intend to be productive if hired. According to one recent empirical study, a record of past publication was the only statistically significant predictor of probability of future publication, as contrasted with, say, whether one had attended an elite school.[11]

The Write Stuff

Publishing good legal scholarship is one way—we would say *the* way—to distinguish yourself as a candidate. In fact it is becoming essential: Many candidates at the AALS will have published one post-law school law review article; many hiring committees now expect prior publication. This represents a dramatic change in hiring from twenty years ago. Having published something after law school will also set you apart from other applicants to elite LL.M. programs, VAPs, and fellowships. Larry Solum suggests that Nonstandard Model candidates publish three articles.

> "Why three?" you ask. Because the AALS form that you will need to fill out leaves room for exactly three articles & you want to have a post-graduation article for each of the three spaces. The hardest part of the process is getting past the initial screen—when members of faculty appointments committees read hundreds and hundreds of AALS forms. Increasingly, their eyes seek out the part of the form with the three publications—so you want to make your best impression right at that moment![12]

But there is another important reason that you should consider writing: It will be a large part of your job as a law professor.[13] At the very least, you will have to satisfy the publication requirements to receive tenure, and many schools now conduct some form of posttenure review, tying productivity to raises, the freedom to teach specialized seminars, and even time and day preferences for classes. And Randy Barnett suggests that "because tenure is so

---

11. Richard E. Redding, "Where Did You Go to Law School?" *Gatekeeping for the Professoriate and Its Implications for Legal Education*, 53 J. LEGAL EDUC. 594 (2003).

12. Lawrence Solum, *Barnett on Entry-Level Academic Jobs*, LEGAL THEORY BLOG (Mar. 10, 2005, 5:21 PM), http://lsolum.blogspot.com/archives/2005_03_01_lsolum_archive/'. html#111049728264231424.

13. Indeed, if you are a Nonstandard Model candidate, you had better enjoy writing, because this particular theory of advancement will require that you produce as much as *double* the amount of scholarship of the Standard Model Elite candidate. That's because it's relatively common that getting tenure will require that you produce three "substantial" works of scholarship—the paradigm is the 25,000-word law review article—*while you are on the faculty*. It's fair to say that even a Standard Model Elite candidate nowadays has to have published at least one article, but that still means four, and not six, on the way to tenure.

easily obtained at most schools," appointments committees are more likely "to judge pre-appointment writings by tenure standards."[14]

Before you go to the stress and expense of getting an LL.M. and going on the job market, you should try writing to see if it really appeals to you. Brad Wendel goes so far as to say that there isn't any such thing as a doctrinal "teaching" job:

> It's really a *writing* job. If you are wondering whether a ~~teaching~~ writing job is for you, try this acid test: Do you have several, maybe even dozens of good ideas for law review articles that you really *have* to write? Do you find yourself reconceptualizing some theoretical question pertaining to law while you're taking a shower? Do cases, articles, or books you read make you mad, make you wonder how seemingly intelligent people can think such silly things? Are you someone, as Max Weber says you must be, who believes that "the fate of his soul depends on whether or not he makes the correct conjecture at this passage of this manuscript"? If the answer to at least one of these questions is yes, you may be enough of a law geek to make it in this profession.[15]

That is not to say that if you find writing difficult, teaching is not for you. Many seasoned professors find writing slow going. The key is whether, despite however quickly or slowly the words flow, you find the subjects you are writing about engaging and stimulating. "[Y]ou should love teaching and try hard to be good at it. But if you do not also have a passion for writing and publishing, then you are dooming yourself to a frustrating teaching career."[16]

How to turn an idea into a published article is beyond the scope of this work. [17] However, we have a few suggestions for getting started.

> ❯ *Read good legal scholarship.* Even academic writers have to find a distinctive voice. Like other writers, beginning academics often imitate the voices of scholars whose work they admire as they attempt to find theirs. If you know what area of law you'll be interested in writing about, get the canonical works in that area and read those articles. In addition, read other academics who have reputations for good style, regardless of subject matter.

> ❯ *Use what you've got.* As mentioned in chapter 1, the best place to begin is to leverage the intellectual capital you already possess. Even if you are practicing in an area that will *not* be your primary area of interest as a teacher, using what you already have is easier than accumulating a whole new knowledge base. If you wrote as a student, either on law review or in

---

14. Barnett, *supra* note 2.

15. Wendel, *supra* note 3, answer after question "What makes a candidate stand out?"

16. Barnett, *supra* note 2.

17. For two excellent guides to writing law review articles, see *supra* chapter 1, note 21.

your classes, see if there is anything that could be used from those prior writings to form part of a more developed article.

> *Create an "idea folder" or notebook.* Always be on the lookout for interesting news items, court cases, and the like that could give rise to articles. Collect these items, perhaps with a note to yourself about why you found it interesting, and file them away. You could also try keeping a notebook of ideas for future articles. Get in the habit of carrying it with you—you never know when inspiration will strike! And if the thought of carrying around a notebook horrifies you, you might rethink this career option, or at least use the note function on your iPhone.

> *Start small.* In addition to demonstrating your commitment to scholarship, writing before you apply to LL.M. programs or register with the AALS gives you practice. Writing law review articles is not intuitive; like all writing, it requires regular effort in order to improve. Just as you would not take up jogging by registering for a marathon, you should not begin your career as a legal scholar attempting to remake a particular field with your first article. That would be frustrating and self-defeating. Even if you have a big idea, consider developing it in a series of smaller articles.[18] (See suggestions in the "Beginning Law Review Article Ideas" box.)

> *Start smaller.* If the idea of beginning a law review article from scratch intimidates you, start even smaller. Many state bar journals provide an excellent forum for practitioner-oriented scholarship. You won't get any credit for it when you go on the market—in fact, you wouldn't even want to list it on your AALS resume form, lest committees get the idea you don't know the difference between academic and nonacademic writing. But a bar journal piece will give you some writing practice, and enable you to ascertain whether you want to write longer, more ambitious pieces. It might also serve as the springboard for that longer, more analytical academic article.

> *Write for credit.* If you are reading this book in law school, petition the school to receive writing credit for as many semesters as possible. These can be directed studies where you work with a professor who will supervise the drafting of a law review article with you. One professor we know did this three times during law school, and had three separate articles or essays drafted by the end of law school.

However you decide to approach it, at some point you have to write those first sentences. Getting the first article written is an important hurdle; we think it's best to write at least one piece *before* you go on the market, when the pressure is not as great as it will be after you are hired and your continued employment will depend, in large part, on the articles you write. We've seen new professors become paralyzed, obsessively rewriting the same piece way

---

18. This is a complex subject. The accepted wisdom is that one's scholarship matures and improves over time, and each of us has that sense about our own work. Despite the predominance of "law and" over doctrine, a solid doctrinal piece on an important issue, making sound normative recommendations for a change in the law, is not a bad strategy for one's first work.

Beginning Law Review Article Ideas

Below are a few suggestions to get you started. Of course, if you already have a theoretically ambitious piece in mind, or if you are confident that you have a big idea you are ready to write up, start work on those. But on the theory that a well-executed *something* beats nothing, we offer the following ideas:

> *Note, comment, or seminar paper redux.* Look back to the writing you did while in law school. Chances are that something you've already started can serve to germinate a broader piece. Take the study you may have already done of one area and update and expand it (maybe a fifty-state survey?), and look for common themes, problems, developing trends, or hopeless tangles. Is there a unifying principle that could make sense of it all?

> *A critical review of doctrine.* Even after a short stint in practice, you will likely encounter some question on which courts have gone in different directions—an issue on which there is a circuit split, for example. Describing the problem, surveying the case law, and either concluding that one set of cases gets the question "right," or that all approaches are wrong and a different approach ought to be adopted, is a great first article, particularly to help litigators used to advocacy writing make the transition to scholarly writing that, in theory at least, is critical, disinterested, and objective.

> *The recent-Supreme-Court-case article.* Another excellent way to begin is to write on a recent Supreme Court case. It should describe the case itself, critically evaluate it, and then look to the implications of the case for the particular area. Does it clarify important questions? Create them? Will it be easy or difficult for lower courts to implement? Is it simply wrong? Outstanding examples of this kind of writing can be found in the *Supreme Court Review*, published annually by the University of Chicago Press, and the *Cato Supreme Court Review*, published annually by the libertarian Cato Institute. The article has to be more than merely a description of the decision, though. Critical analysis of the case is key.

> *The book review essay.* Law review book reviews are longer than those appearing in other academic journals, but still much shorter than a normal article (a good length is fifteen to twenty pages, though some run even longer). The advantage in reviewing a book is that you really don't have to come up with ideas yourself; you are merely critiquing someone else's. Further, for the beginner, book reviews are often good opportunities to survey the literature in the field as you situate the book under review in that area. Be aware, though, that the review needs to be something more than merely a book report. You will need to critically engage the work; to do that well may require either some preexisting knowledge about the subject, or a crash course in the canonical works to obtain that knowledge. If the latter, your time may be better spent on a different project.

beyond the point of added value. Everyone has to start somewhere; you will look back on early articles and see things you would do differently. But that's the point: Your scholarship will improve over the life of your career, but you have to write something to begin that process.

If you are currently in law school and are contemplating teaching as a profession, we would urge you to take upper-level courses in which papers are either required or an option. Use that opportunity to produce a paper of truly publishable quality, and *tell your professor that's what you intend*. Even if you've already published a note or comment in your law review, research the journals—and there are more than you think—that will accept student work, or wait to submit until you've graduated. For most of us, the ability to involve students in that part of our jobs is exciting, and you might be surprised by how much your professor will help you. While this might mean that you work on the paper even *after* you've received your grade, the future payoff is immeasurable. The same applies to LL.M. programs: Make the most of your writing opportunities and view every paper as a potential publication.

There is a final question that you might have at this point: Can writing alone obviate the need for an elite LL.M., saving you substantial amounts of money and time? The answer is, "It depends." In large part, we think, it depends on the reputation of the school from which you received your J.D. and, frankly, what you've done since graduation. If you went to a well-regarded (but not elite) public or private law school, did very well, were a law review editor, and are at a prestigious national firm (see the list of "merit badges" above), then you might be able to publish a couple of articles and receive interviews at the AALS. You should know that the schools from which you will likely receive interviews will probably be ranked significantly lower than your law school alma mater. You would probably do much better—both in quantity and quality of schools—if you added the LL.M. to your credentials mix. But there are exceptions—one of Denning and McCormick's former colleagues was hired two years after she graduated from a state law school, in large part on the strength of the four (!) articles she had published since graduation and the extensive research agenda she presented at the interview. Another of their friends, who graduated from a school then in the third tier of *U.S. News & World Report*'s rankings, received a tenure track job after several short-term teaching positions. He has written several books, more than ten articles, and several other scholarly pieces. Therefore, if you can get the job you want without paying for school, then there's no need to spend the money. Wait and publish two or three good articles and go on the market. If you don't get a job, then apply to an LL.M. program.

But don't just take our word for it. Many others who give advice on how to get a job in law teaching likewise emphasize the importance of writing. Brad Wendel says that "the three most important things an aspiring law professor can do is publish, publish, publish."[19] And in the same vein, Larry Solum suggests

---

19. Wendel, *supra* note 3, answer after question "Why are law schools so fixated on prestige?"

Write! Write! Write! The entry-level market in changing. Two of the four entry-level offers made by [the University of San Diego in 2005] were to candidates with monographs published by prestigious academic presses and multiple articles in scholarly journals. If your JD is from an institution that does not place significant numbers of graduates in entry-level academic positions, then writing is all the more significant.[20]

Getting the Elite LL.M.

Several elite schools, notably Harvard, Yale, and Columbia, offer LL.M. graduate degrees. A significant number of enrollees to these programs will come from abroad, but some American students who are preparing for a teaching career are also admitted. The LL.M. is usually a one-year program[21] in which the student takes classes offered at the law school and may write a thesis as a requirement to graduate. The purpose is not so much to increase one's store of legal knowledge, but as it is often put, to "launder" one's non-elite school degree. The Ivy League credential will signal seriousness of intent, and will furnish one of those proxies that gives appointments committees some comfort (warranted or not) about the intellectual ability of the candidate.

Ideally, LL.M. programs permit you to take courses from renowned professors and get a sense of how big-time legal academia works. Many elite law schools have seminars on academic legal writing and other courses specifically designed for those desiring to enter the teaching profession. Further, spending time at an elite law school—even for only a year—can be an excellent networking opportunity. Many of your classmates, and many of the J.D. students you encounter, will eventually teach. These will be valuable contacts for the future. In addition, LL.M. programs, theoretically at least, offer the opportunity to write—either because they require a thesis as a condition of graduation, because courses will offer paper options that can be expanded into publications, or because you can do an independent study under the supervision of a faculty member. And if nothing else, an LL.M. provides an opportunity to internalize the norms of academia, especially if it has been a few years since receiving your J.D.

You should be aware, however, that LL.M. programs have their drawbacks. They are expensive, both in terms of out-of-pocket expenses like tuition and room and board, and in opportunity costs, like foregone income. These costs may be a particular hardship to applicants with families. LL.M. programs are often cash cows for law schools, moreover, so don't expect much

---

20. Solum, *supra* note 12.

21. Columbia designates some of its graduate students "Associates-in-Law." These students are in residence for two years, receive a tuition waiver and stipend, and teach an introductory class, either in legal writing or the introduction to American law course taught to foreign students. The associates may or may not receive a graduate degree when they complete their term.

in the way of financial aid to help with tuition. It is likely that you will be subsidizing the aid given to a J.D. candidate!

An LL.M. from an elite school is *not* the equivalent of a J.D. from the same school; no one knows that better than professors at those schools. Therefore, do not expect that faculty members will fall all over themselves mentoring you. As an LL.M. student, you may have to endure some embarrassing encounters with prominent professors who do not view you as worthy of their time. There *are* some who will agree to work with aspiring professors, however humble that student's pedigree; you may just have to knock on several doors to find them.

Do not overestimate the time that you will have to write. If you plan to go on the job market during your LL.M. year—which is what many candidates will do—then you will likely submit your information to the AALS *before* you attend a single class! Your fall semester will be a whirlwind of classes, interviewing at the AALS conference, and (one hopes) trips to schools on callback interviews. That will not leave much time for sustained research and writing, which is an argument for either substantially finishing at least one post-law school writing project before beginning the program, applying for a fellowship after your LL.M. year instead of immediately going on the market, or both. An LL.M. program can help you sharpen your interests and set an agenda for the future. Writing papers for classes may also give you a head start on that agenda, as well as creating more opportunities to get feedback on your ideas and your writing from your professors. If you haven't been able to publish much, and you have a choice, you might strongly consider programs that require a thesis for graduation.

"Sounds good," you might be thinking, "so which LL.M. programs count as 'elite' and will serve the non-elite-J.D.-laundering-function and how do I get admitted?" First, we want to be clear that specialized LL.M. programs, that is, those that purport to provide specialized training in a topic like health law or environmental law and that are sometimes offered by non-elite schools, will generally *not* offer any appreciable benefit at the AALS. Some exceptions to this rule include an LL.M. in tax from a nationally recognized program like those at New York University, Georgetown, or Florida, which is now de rigueur for tax practitioners and academics alike.[22] Additionally, Stanford has a good track record of training and placing minority candidates through its LL.M. and S.J.D. programs.

As for admissions requirements, each school is different, but in general, the schools favor candidates who appear serious about teaching as a career, and who are likely to be successful candidates on the job market. These schools are interested in admitting those who had good grades in law school, but they are also going to weigh heavily any publications you already have, your personal statement, and recommendations—especially recommendations from

---

22. For an excellent guide to tax LL.M. programs, see Paul L. Caron, Jennifer M. Kowal & Katherine Pratt, *Pursuing a Tax LLM Degree: Why and When* (Univ. of Cincinnati Public Law Research Paper No. 10-11; Loyola-LA Legal Studies Paper No. 2010-9), http://ssrn.com/abstract=1577966.

law professors who can say something about your potential as a candidate. It is vitally important if you are considering applying to an LL.M. program that you contact former professors whose classes you had (and did well in) about your plans and ask if they would feel comfortable writing a recommendation. Many schools strongly suggest at least one such recommendation; we think that nearly all should come from academics, either those for whom you did substantial work as undergraduates or former law professors.

If you didn't form close relationships with your professors in law school, it is not too late to start! You can try e-mailing a former professor and explain your plans, ask for advice, and even ask the professor to read over your draft personal statement or draft manuscripts (though maybe not all in the initial e-mail). Another option is to start at the top: Many law schools are now creating "dean of scholarship" or "director of faculty development" positions. These are faculty who have an interest in assisting faculty in the production and dissemination of scholarship and raising the profile and reputation of the law school in the process. Because having alumni in the academy also raises a law school's profile, we think that you will find such folks eager to assist potential candidates in a variety of ways. Remember, too, that it is especially helpful if you establish relationships with your former professors who are graduates of the schools to which you will be applying. Law schools like hearing from their alums in academia, and their weighing in on your behalf may carry some additional weight.

The personal statement is also going to be very important in admissions decisions. Ordinarily the personal statement will ask you to describe your interest in teaching and your research interests in three to five pages. This is good practice in two ways: First, the "why do you want to teach" question is one you will encounter when you interview at the AALS and it is always a surprise how poor some candidates' responses are; second, writing the personal statement will force you to focus on what it is that you want to write about when you become a professor. This, in turn, makes it easier to actually focus enough to begin each writing project. Serious, focused reflection, no matter at what stage in your career, is always a good exercise.

For both questions, specificity is always better than vague generalization, and positives about the academy trump negatives about practice. Be able to describe precisely why teaching, as opposed to staying in practice, appeals to you. Be sure to *avoid* any answer that sounds like you are simply tired of practice and figure that law professors have a much more congenial work schedule. Similarly, when you describe what you want to write about, avoid both answers that are too general ("I want to study law as an instrument of social change") or too grandiose ("I plan to work on a comprehensive theory of constitutional interpretation rooted in Kantian moral philosophy"). By the time that you fill out your applications to LL.M. programs, you ought to be able to describe, at least in a paragraph or two, a writing project that you have conceived (if not yet executed).

Your personal statement should also say something about why you are applying to a program at a particular school. Does it have faculty from whom you especially want to take classes? Is it known for its focus on law and economics, public law, international law, or some other area in which you hope to teach? Show that you know something about the school—that you aren't just throwing applications at every school in the top ten hoping someone will let you in. It's a lot of effort to do this kind of work up front, but it will greatly enhance your chances of success. That kind of effort, moreover, is precisely what makes a good teacher and scholar.

If getting the LL.M. is something that is important to you, you should *agonize* over the personal statement—it may be some of the most important writing you ever do. This is your chance to convey a sense of what makes you unique, and what you will bring to the class that other potential admittees will not. If you have something in your background that makes you unique, or that would provide any sort of diversity to the class—especially if it is not an obvious quality—use the personal statement to highlight that. This is your shot to differentiate yourself from the hundreds of applications the admissions committee will be reviewing.

Does S.J.D. Mean J-O-B?

Academics in disciplines other than law are often surprised ("scandalized" might be a better word) that many legal academics possess only a J.D. and that graduate studies in law don't exist in the same sense that they exist in other disciplines. In fact, there is a terminal degree in law beyond the LL.M.; it is the "Doctor of Juridical Science" (abbreviated S.J.D. or J.S.D. at most schools). "Well, if one graduate degree is good," you might be thinking, "why not get two?" The simple answer is that it is very likely unnecessary, and may even hurt you.

Explaining that counterintuitive observation requires some explanation of what an S.J.D. is, and what it is not. While it is technically the terminal degree in American graduate legal studies, it usually is *not* the equivalent of a humanities or social science Ph.D. Those programs usually require extensive graduate-level coursework, followed by comprehensive examination, and a book-length dissertation. Ph.D. candidates also have teaching responsibilities, giving them some experience designing lessons, administering and grading exams, and so on. S.J.D.s, on the other hand, usually require no additional coursework beyond that required for an LL.M.[23]—there are often few residence requirements. At many schools you simply have to find several law professors to be on your dissertation committee and write a long-ish (but not necessarily book-length) paper (sometimes a series of papers will suffice). There are usually no teaching opportunities associated with S.J.D. programs.

In most cases, if your goal is to be taken seriously as a candidate, an elite LL.M. will suffice. The S.J.D. would be like gilding the lily. If you are unsuccessful the first time through for a permanent position, you should investigate the growing number of fellowships and VAPs—both discussed below—as a way to build your resume and, more important, as a way to beef

---

23. An LL.M. is usually a prerequisite, and some schools will entertain S.J.D. applications *only* from graduates of that school's LL.M. program.

up your bibliography. Further, for American students, getting the S.J.D. may raise concerns about being "too academic" for some law schools. (Recall the "Law and Basket Weaving" skeptics described above.) There may be perfectly good reasons why you would want to pursue the S.J.D. degree, but you should not do so thinking that it will enhance your marketability. As is true with an LL.M., getting an S.J.D. won't be looked on as the equivalent of having gotten your J.D. at an elite school in the first place.

The reference in the prior paragraph to "American students" brings us to an important qualification of what we have just said about the S.J.D. Because law degrees in other countries are often undergraduate degrees, foreign candidates who wish to teach in the United States will likely find it advisable to complete an S.J.D. at an elite American law school to be competitive at the AALS.

Fellowships and VAPs

A number of schools, both elite and not, have increasingly been offering fellowships or VAP positions specifically designed to help people get into tenure track positions elsewhere. Some of them have been around for quite some time, like the Bigelow Fellowship at the University of Chicago, and the VAP at Chicago-Kent. In recent years, more schools, like Northwestern, have developed fellowships or VAPs geared primarily for their own graduates, but also open to others. Their proliferation, in fact, is one of the biggest changes in the law school hiring process over the last decade. University of Cincinnati Professor Paul Caron maintains an updated list on his blog.[24] At last count, there were nearly seventy fellowship and VAP programs run by dozens of different law schools.

There are essentially two models of fellowship or VAP, and these titles are used interchangeably, so by themselves, they reveal little. All of these programs share some common attributes: They last for a short term, usually one or two years; they give the participants the opportunity to teach at least one class; they give participants the ability to attend faculty workshops; and they give participants the opportunity to write, with greater access to scholars who can provide valuable feedback. In addition, participants have free access to computerized databases like Westlaw and Lexis, proximity to a law library, and a guest office with a computer—all of which are quite helpful to novice scholars! Generally, fellows and VAPs have a lighter class load, a much smaller salary, less institutional support, and no prospects of continued employment beyond the short term as compared to their tenure-track colleagues. Many are also allowed to participate in faculty meetings and serve on at least some faculty committees, most often without any sort of vote.

From there, the models diverge, although there may be some overlap. One model, the Junior Doctrinal Prof model, treats the participants much like regular faculty members in that they teach only in doctrinal areas and may have a specialized seminar. The other model, the Legal Writing Prof model,

---

24. *See Fellowships for Aspiring Law Professors*, TaxProf Blog (Aug. 31, 2010), http://taxprof.typepad.com/taxprof_blog/2010/08/fellowships-for-aspiring.html.

rticipants teach first-year law students legal analysis, research, and
hese folks may also have the opportunity to teach a doctrinal class
.

As you can see, the fellowship or VAP route has some real advantages.
Basically, it's an opportunity to try out law teaching, to write, to network, and
to internalize the norms of legal academia. There are some downsides as well,
however. Because most of these are very short term, you might have to go on
the job market at the same time you start. As for writing, similar to where you
would find yourself in pursuing an LL.M., you are best off already having at
least one article done before you start. Additionally, because the first (or second) time teaching can be so time intensive, you will find that you don't have
nearly the time you expected to devote to scholarship.

This is triply true if you pursue a Legal Writing model opportunity. It
is nearly impossible to write at the same time that you are teaching writing,
because teaching writing is so labor intensive and requires so much individual
feedback for students. Moreover, some appointments committees look down
on those who have pursued Legal Writing model opportunities (Chicago's
Bigelow and Harvard's Climenko Fellows are notable exceptions to this) for
the same reasons that doctrinal faculty members sometimes look down on
skills faculty. Candidates may have to explain away the legal writing portion
of their position.

And your writing is still the most important part of this opportunity. We
know of many Fellows and VAPs who went on to tenure-track jobs, but also
many who did not. The more successful folks wrote more, earned LL.M.s
at elite schools, or both. And if those hurdles weren't enough, getting a law
teaching job is becoming so competitive that those we consider Standard
Model candidates are using these stepping stones in greater numbers. Some
candidates for fellowships or VAPs will have already published, in fact, and in
a drive to place people more successfully, those hiring for these positions are
starting to look for publications as an indicator of future scholarly success, just
as for tenure track positions.

These caveats aside, however, a fellowship or a VAP is a great opportunity and in many ways offers more substance than an LL.M. from an elite
school. Just keep in mind that for most, the Junior Doctrinal Prof model will
provide greater advantages than will the Legal Writing Prof model. But even
the Legal Writing Prof model, depending on the institution, is in many ways
better than pursuing another degree because you will get valuable teaching
experience and the school will pay you, rather than the other way around.
And more schools are becoming much better at marketing their programs, the
participants in their programs, and their graduates, because in the end, it all
benefits the schools.

Pleased to Meat You, Hope You Guess My Name: Preparing for (and Surviving) the AALS Hiring Conference

Because we're professors, we cannot help, before we get to the practical stuff, speculating about some of the deeper mysteries of the Association of American Law Schools' annual hiring conference, affectionately (in a love/hate sort of way) known to those who participate as the "meat market." Just how and why did this highly efficient but grueling institution come to be? Here is a thesis. Doctoral programs in the humanities and sciences seek to place their graduates as entry-level professors in a college or university; that's the whole point of getting a Ph.D. in history or philosophy or English![1] Law schools, on the other hand, are primarily designed to train lawyers (and help them find jobs as such), and the restocking of the law faculty gene pool is something of a side business. Grad students in the humanities and sciences have a number of years to network within their professional associations (like the American Philosophical Association), use resources like the *Chronicle of Higher Education*, and attend meetings very similar to the meat market.

We don't think, however, that there's anything in university hiring on the scale of the AALS Faculty Recruitment Conference (FRC), and we're willing to speculate that its existence is the natural result of the fact that most (not all) law faculty hiring has, historically, been a small in-migration from the practice of law. That also perhaps accounts for the culture shock: Even assuming history, philosophy, or physics departments do something akin to the FRC, the interviewers and the interviewees would already share a common academic culture. Add a soupçon of confusion and physical exhaustion to the culture shock, as some thousand or so interviewers, representing about 200 schools, gather in one large hotel to meet some five hundred or so interviewees in half-hour slots over two days, and you can start to appreciate why incumbent professors are so happy they never have to do it again.

So, as you will see, whatever its genesis and however grueling, the AALS hiring process is efficient at bringing together those who seek entry-level hires

---

1. The dean of graduate programs at one of the two or three leading research universities in the country told one of us (casually, at a dinner) that his decisions about how many students a particular discipline may admit to the Ph.D. program in a given year is directly related to his view of the eventual job prospects for those admittees.

H C

who want entry-level teaching jobs. *The vast majority of entry-level* *ne here, so it is essential that you understand how the process works.* *rith an overview of the process, and then examine each step in that process in detail. We devote chapter 4 to postconference events, like callback interviews at schools with whom you have interviewed, and chapter 5 to special concerns of particular groups of candidates

AN OVERVIEW OF THE AALS PROCESS

Traditionally, the AALS hiring conference has taken place during the last part of October and sometimes as late as the first week in November. Since many schools now wish to conclude their entry-level hiring prior to the break for the December holidays, the hiring conference may be moving earlier in October. It runs from Thursday through Sunday, with most interviews being conducted all day Friday and Saturday. In recent years, the conference has taken place in Washington, D.C., at the Marriott Wardman Park hotel.

Your work, however, will begin much earlier. The summer prior to the conference, usually at the beginning of August, you will register with the AALS as a candidate, pay a fee, and fill out a standard online resume form that will go in the Faculty Appointments Register (FAR). Those forms will be posted on the AALS's Web site, along with your resume (or as you will learn to call it, your "CV"—curriculum vitae). There will be four distributions of these to participating schools, but, for reasons described below, *you will want to be in the first distribution.* Hiring committees will begin poring over the FAR in August or September, after the first distribution, and will schedule interviews at thirty-minute intervals at the hiring conference with candidates they wish to interview.

At these hiring conference screening interviews, you will be questioned by members of the appointments committee on a variety of topics and will have the opportunity to ask questions about the law school and its programs. At the end of the weekend, the committees will decide to fly back a small number of candidates whom the committee feels best fit the school. As we will detail in chapter 4, during these callbacks, you will speak with more faculty, give a presentation (the "job talk"), and will often meet with representatives of the university (unless, of course, the law school is a stand-alone law school, not part of a larger university). An offer will then be made following conversations among the committee, the faculty, and, of course, the dean.

THE FAR

If you go to the AALS Web site (http://www.aals.org/frs/frc.php) you will find information about the Conference and the FAR itself. The fee listed on the site covers distribution of your FAR form to schools as well as registration for the Conference. By following the directions on the Web site, you will be able to fill in twenty-two fields in the FAR form—education,

Sample FAR Form

1. Name		5. Personal Data
2. Phone	*(Work) (Home) (*Pref)	Gender: Race:
3. Fax/E-mail	Fax: E-mail:	
4. Address		
4a. Alt. Address		
6. 1st Law Degree	School: Date:	
7. Law School Honors	(a) Rank: (b) Law Review: (c) Other Law Honors:	
8. Advanced Law Degrees		
8a. Other Advanced Degrees		
9. Undergraduate Education	School(s) & Degrees: Honors:	
10. Law School- Teaching Experience	[School if applicable]: Position: Subjects: Comments:	
11. Other Teaching Experience		
12. Subjects Most Like to Teach	1: [Select options from a drop-down menu for each choice] 2: 3: Comments:	
13. Other Subjects May Be Interested in Teaching	1: [Select options from a drop-down menu for each choice] 2: 3: 4: Comments:	
14. Other Subjects Would Be Willing to Teach, if Asked	1: [Select options from a drop-down menu for each choice] 2: 3: 4: Comments:	
15. Geographic Restrictions		
16. Employment	Type: Employer/Location: Position/Description: Dates of Employment: ___ You may [not] contact my employer. Type: Employer/Location: Position/Description: Dates of Employment: ___ You may [not] contact my employer.	
17. Major Published Writings		
18. Bar Admissions		
19. References		
20. Comments		
21. Date Available		22. Resume

experience, publication, and so on. The effect is that every candidate's submission is identically formatted.

Make sure you understand the implication of this uniformity. At many law schools, you can identify the members of the Faculty Appointments Committee in late August and September, because someone has printed out all 1,000 FAR forms and bound them to resemble the Manhattan White Pages, and the committee members lug them around in order to use every spare five minutes to complete their screening review assignments. Because (1) the format is uniform; (2) the amount of information that you can provide is limited, objective, and brief; and (3) committee members generally make very quick "up or down" decisions while skimming through the FAR forms very quickly, you want to maximize the impact your form will have. Because you want to maximize *positive* impact, moreover, the first rule is that whatever you put on your FAR, the form should be proofread within an inch of its life!

Think very carefully about how you can demonstrate, within the limited constraints of the form, that you will be a productive and contributing colleague. In addition to listing the usual credentials, think about the courses that you are willing to teach and about how to signal your potential as a scholar. Look for areas of overlap within subjects you are willing to teach and between those and areas in which you plan to write. It may seem like a lot of work, but the reflection that it takes to frame your worth and articulate your goals will serve you well in a career that has fewer external validators than most jobs. Additionally, considering the needs of your audience will help you be a better teacher and scholar.

And so, to make the most of the limitations of the FAR form, there are a few fields that warrant special attention:

> *Education.* There is a space for Rank. If your school ranked you, put it. Otherwise it looks as if you're hiding the fact you didn't do well. And for heaven's sake, if your law school *did* rank its students, don't put down that it didn't.

> *Subjects Most Like to Teach/May Be Interested in Teaching/Would be Willing to Teach, if Asked.* You should give considerable thought to what you want to teach, and what you would be *willing* to teach. It is likely that you have a strong preference for one or two classes—usually, those in which you've done some writing or with which you are familiar from practice. But remember, at most law schools, you will be teaching *four* classes a year, and you have to think about the needs of the school. Be specific; often, there are first-year classes like civil procedure or property that need staffing. Commercial law, tax, criminal law, evidence, and professional responsibility (legal ethics) are also perennial needs at many law schools. As you consider the choices to put down, don't forget that it's not necessary that you write in *every* subject that you would teach. And while it is important that you be able to articulate how your courses relate to one another and to your scholarly agenda, that relationship need be neither perfect nor obvious.[2] This will be discussed more below, in the section on the interview.

---

2. Faculties vary in their desire to have professors write and teach in the same areas. Some schools simply don't care if the writing has anything to do with the subjects you teach. Some do. That will tend to come out as the interviews progress. This, of course, raises the

> *Geographic Restrictions.* There are undoubtedly some cases in which it is imperative that you restrict your search to a particular area of the country. But if you are not in a situation like that, to maximize your chances, you should indicate no restrictions. You may have a strong preference to stay where you currently live, but you are handicapping your appeal if you let schools in on this. And you're potentially selling yourself short on the opportunity to explore areas of the country that have more to offer than you thought. Do not be like the candidate a few years ago whose FAR form expressed a willingness to accept jobs only in "Blue" states, as opposed to "Red" ones; or like candidates who indicate they will not accept a position in Alaska, which has no law school. There's also the issue of the impression a highly selective designation makes on the committee member. A recruiting committee chair once told one of us that a candidate's being picky geographically showed that he or she wasn't really willing to do what it takes to become a law professor. Remember: As long as you are operating in good faith, and have not concluded irrevocably that you would never take the job under any circumstance, you can always turn down the interview, the callback, or the job offer.[3]

> *Employment.* There will be a place for you to indicate whether schools can contact your employer. Committees are often very good about checking references, both those you supply and "off-list" references, including people committee members may know at firms where you've worked, and sometimes before the initial screening interview. If you haven't told your employer that you're a candidate, then be sure to leave this box unchecked.

> *Major Published Writings.* This means what it says. Limit these to major published writings: scholarly articles, books, chapters, and other sections of books or treatises. There's room here for three, and if you have more than three, put the most recent ones. Use the full cite if they're published; SSRN links may lead readers to conclude the writings are unpublished or in progress. If you have more than three substantial pieces, you can list earlier writings if there's some reason to showcase them, that is, if you got a fantastic placement, it's on a particularly hot topic, or it has been cited a great deal. Remember, you'll be able to upload your CV, and committee members will be able to print that along with your FAR form.

> *References.* As mentioned in chapter 2, at least one of these should be a law professor who could attest to your suitability for an academic position. Never put someone down whom you have not contacted in advance, and be sure that those you do list will give you a good recommendation.

---

additional question how much you should puff or pander just to get a job. Our advice: Don't promise or intimate anything you don't intend to do. If you want the job so badly that you *will* write on cutting-edge issues in security interests in investment accounts under UCC Articles 8 and 9, even though you're not quite sure what that means, feel free to intimate away. Otherwise, stick to a story that reasonably approximates the truth.

3. Just to make this a little more concrete, one of us, a lifelong Midwesterner, would have never considered the West Coast until discovering during screening interview due diligence that Sacramento was considered by some to be the "Des Moines of the Central Valley." Unfortunately, Pacific McGeorge never called back.

If you have any doubts, leave that person off your list. And for law professor references, when you ask that person to be a reference, you might ask him or her to review your FAR form and make suggestions.

> *Comments.* There is a space for comments at the bottom. These should be helpful to the committee; it isn't an opportunity to say how much you think your background and experience will make you an excellent teacher, or that you are a team player and a people person. Instead, use it to describe (briefly) a work-in-progress (or more than one), or list a Web site you created for your job search on which you could put future works, your research agenda, your CV, and any other helpful information. Or you could always just leave it blank!

> *Resume.* In a change from prior years, you may upload your CV to the AALS Web site. You should do this in light of the limited space on the FAR form. Committees often review both. Note that a resume and the academic CV, aimed as they are at completely different audiences, look different. To see how a friend transformed Lipshaw's professional resume into an appropriate CV, see Appendix C.

The forms will be distributed four times during an academic year: August, September, October, and a final distribution in February. You will want to fill this out as soon as possible and make sure that your FAR form will be included in the first distribution, the second one at the absolute latest. Many schools will fill their hiring conference interview slots completely with the first distribution. By October, few spots, if any, are left. Rightly or wrongly, most committees assume that the strongest, most committed candidates are in the first distribution.

SUPPLEMENTS TO THE FAR

In general, the FAR and the hiring conference are the only games in town for securing a position at an accredited law school. Along with the Standard Model Non-Elite Candidate described in chapter 2, the days of law schools recruiting downtown lawyers have largely come to an end. Even lower-tier schools tend to recruit their tenure-track faculty exclusively from the AALS. Thus, we were careful to label this section "supplements to" the FAR, instead of "substitutes for" the FAR and the AALS. That said, there are a few additional ways you can market your candidacy, in hopes of standing out.

Direct Contact

Once you register with the AALS, you will receive access to the Job Bulletin, which lists ads from schools for positions on their faculty. The hiring committees from these schools will be combing through the AALS, but if there are schools whose curricular needs are a particularly good fit, you can always send a letter to the chair of the hiring committee, who is usually listed in the ad itself. You should include a brief cover letter indicating your interest in interviewing with them at the hiring conference, a copy of your CV, and reprints of your articles. The cover letter should indicate anything that might make you a particularly attractive candidate for that school—ties to the area, good fit with courses, and the like. If the committee has already flagged you as someone they wish to talk to, your follow up will reinforce their initial sense that you are a candidate worth a closer look. If they haven't, then your making contact may spur someone to take a second look. Honestly, we can't think of a single downside to this, assuming the substance of your direct contact doesn't persuade a committee that already wants to see you into dropping you from the interview list. So whatever you send, make it good!

School-Specific Registers

Many schools will bind the CVs of their graduates or those enrolled in their graduate programs and distribute those to schools interviewing at the AALS. If you are a graduate of a school that does this, you will want to find out when these are bound and distributed so that you can ensure yours is included. If you don't know whom to contact, a good place to start is either the career services office or, perhaps, the dean of scholarship (if the school has one), who could put you on the right track. We suspect that these have declined somewhat in influence, since all candidates can upload complete CVs to the FAR Web site, but being included may catch the eye of a committee member who prefers, for one reason or another, to look at candidates from a select school or group of schools—school snobs, in other words.

Creating a Web Site

When one of us (Denning) went on the job market in 1998—before the availability of online submission of the FAR form and CV—his wife designed a simple Web site containing a complete CV, copies of publications, a research agenda, and a statement about why he wanted to teach. He placed the Web site address (his wife had reserved his name as a domain name) in the "Comments" section of the FAR form and invited committee members to visit there for more information. According to the Web site's logs, this generated a significant amount of traffic, particularly before the AALS conference and prior to callback interviews. Several interviewers mentioned that they had visited the Web site, and its content provided the basis for a number of good conversations.

What is surprising is how few law candidates do this (our sense is that candidates in other disciplines do this somewhat more regularly). It can be a great supplement to the "cold record" provided in the FAR, allowing the committee to get a better sense of who you are and what you might bring to the faculty.

Note, however, for the job search, the Web site should be all business. Your MySpace or Facebook page with pictures of your pets or your whitewater-rafting vacation is not going to be very helpful. In fact, you might consider taking down your MySpace or Facebook page during your job search, especially if it has pictures or comments that might be considered offensive or that show you engaged in questionable behavior. The same goes for any blogs you might have or to which you contribute (even in the comments section) regularly. Committees are getting savvy about these things, as are all employers, so let the candidate beware.

THE FACULTY RECRUITMENT CONFERENCE

Scheduling the Conference Interview

A couple of weeks or so after the first distribution, if all has gone well, you should be receiving calls or e-mails from hiring committees asking you to interview with them in Washington. Ordinarily, you will be asked to schedule an interview for that weekend. You should keep careful track of when you scheduled the interview, and with whom. If it is a school in which you are particularly interested, and you have a choice, you might want to schedule it for earlier in the morning, when you and the committee are both at your freshest. If possible, avoid scheduling late afternoon interviews when you, and the committee, are going to be flagging. Try to keep some spaces open for breaks, too, if possible.

There's some lore, albeit untested empirically, about scheduling. Supposedly the best times are Friday afternoon (but not the last slot before cocktails), after the committee has gotten settled in, and Saturday morning before everybody completely loses it as things wrap up. Who knows? Lipshaw relates this anecdote: He had become a cyberfriend of a very accomplished professor at a particular school, who, as it turned out, happened also to be the chair of the appointments committee for the 2005 FRC. About ten days before the FRC, she called to tell him that in fact the committee was interested in seeing him. The problem was that the committee only had time slots left at 8:30 AM and 3:30 PM on Saturday. His friend offered these two times, but he already had an interview booked in the morning. So he said, "I will take the afternoon interview, but on the condition that I promise to supply the energy." The two of them chuckled together about that.

Lipshaw thought the interview went swimmingly. People complimented his work. People smiled and nodded. But he did not hear back from his friend. After the New Year, he called her. After an uncomfortable moment, she said, "It really didn't go well at all. A number of the committee members thought you were hyper and unfocused."

On the other hand, Lipshaw's successful screening interview with the school at which he ultimately landed took place the next year on Saturday at 2:30 PM with only two of the committee members left (the others had to catch trains or planes) and one of them was almost comatose on account of a horrendous cold and flu. The point is this: Interviews are a lot like law school exams. Sometimes the ones you thought you bombed, you aced—and vice versa. Your appeal to a particular committee hinges on a lot of variables. All you can do is prepare in advance and be yourself.

When you talk to the hiring chair, be sure to ask if there is material the school usually sends to candidates; most schools do as a matter of course, but make sure that you get whatever information packet the school sends. In particular, get the names of the other members on the hiring committee, so that you could check their CVs and bibliographies. Being able to talk in a bit of detail about them and their interests (avoid, however, so much detail that you sound somewhat creepy) will signal that you've done your homework. It also may provide valuable information to you. For example, if someone on the committee has written in your area, you will likely get questions from that person on any articles that you've published. You, in turn, should send them all the materials you would like *them* to have, including reprints, drafts of articles not yet published, extra CVs, and the like.

Make sure you have a written (or e-mail) confirmation of the time slot. One of us did not for one interview and showed up at 9:30 AM on Saturday instead of 9:30 AM on Friday, missing the chance to interview with an attractive school. While he was absolutely sure that it was the school's mistake and not his, the fact that he had not received a written confirmation should have been a warning sign. If the school has not followed up by the week before the hiring conference, it's not a bad idea to initiate a confirmation on your own behalf.

The Ideal Number of Interviews

Traditional meat market lore treats the interview schedule something like a dance card. The ideal has you never sitting down. And some (including the AALS itself) suggest that if you have fewer than some number of interviews scheduled, you shouldn't even attend the conference. Certainly, if you are able to schedule in the neighborhood of ten to twelve interviews over the weekend, your chances for converting at least some of those interviews into invitations for campus visits are higher. You will overhear candidates complaining about having twenty or more interviews. Ignore them. Remember, you can accept only one job.

And if you're on the other end of the spectrum, don't make any decisions based on the number of interviews you have scheduled. We think that even if you have a small number of interviews, say, fewer than five, you should still consider going. Since you can only take one job, you should attend the conference even if you have a single interview! One of us (McCormick) did not ever have more than five interviews. Even if none of the interviews results in callbacks, you will still have gained valuable interviewing experience for the next time. Moreover, it is a valuable networking opportunity, not only with interviewing schools, but also with other candidates. Although it is a bit rare, you may get impromptu chances to speak with members of the hiring committees or even an additional more formal interview at the conference itself. (We know of at least one current professor who got an offer to interview based on an elevator conversation at the conference!) And as long as you stay away from those candidates who must constantly talk about how great they are and how many interviews they have, you'll meet people a lot like you, and you can develop a pretty good support network through the experience.

Traveling to the Conference

Register early enough to get a room at the hotel (nothing is worse than trying to make it to interviews from other hotels, although staying across the street at the Omni Shoreham is not so bad and may even be preferable for some who wish to avoid the angst in the air at the Wardman Park and uncomfortable elevator rides with appointments committee members and other candidates) and arrive early enough on Thursday that you can relax, reconnoiter the interview suites you'll be visiting the next day, and get a good night's sleep. If the weather is nice, Rock Creek Park is a great place to take a walk. There are also a number of pretty good restaurants around the hotel. Even if you're still working, try to arrange your schedule so that you can focus only on the conference for those two days. Your work will be there when you get back—but not for long, we hope!

Preinterview Recon

The Marriott Wardman Park is a sprawling hotel, full of separate towers, wings, and a bewildering array of room numbers. You will not have much time between interviews. You may be late to one or two. *It is essential that you take some time the night before to familiarize yourself with the hotel layout so that you don't waste time searching for rooms during the interview days.*[4] One of us (McCormick) did that, and still managed to wait outside of the wrong room for an interview. She arrived five minutes late, huffing and puffing. Because she was eight months pregnant, the committee graciously accepted her apology, assuming that the walk from another interview had been too much. Don't count on the hugely pregnant excuse very often, though, and probably never if you're male.

The Interview with the Committee

You'll find that the format for interviews is pretty standard. You will show up at the appointed time, be ushered into the interviewing suite, and after some brief small talk (where you're from, whether you had certain professors in law

---

4. Specifically, there are three towers in the hotel, each with its own elevator bank. The Central Tower is closest to the lobby, and "0" is always the second digit of the room number (e.g., 1017 or 8048). The Park Tower is at least a five-minute walk from the Central Tower through the lobby (not counting the time spent trying to get on an elevator), and past all the ballrooms, almost to the Shoreham Hotel across Calvert Street. The Wardman Tower is a good five minutes the other way from the Central Tower, through a breezeway back toward Connecticut Avenue. Our experience was that most (but not all) interviewing suites were in the Central Tower, with the Wardman Tower second, and the Park Tower last. Having your room in the Central Tower is therefore a big benefit. Also, consider using the stairs and not the elevators. This is no joke. There is a huge crush at about five minutes of the hour and the half-hour, and elevators can break down.

school) you will be asked a series of questions.[5] We'll identify the usual subjects in a minute, but first, we want to summarize what your goal should be in these interviews. This is your chance to demonstrate your value in a way that paper alone cannot. You want to be memorable (in a good way) to a committee that will likely be interviewing up to thirty candidates over two days. Dan Solove has summarized seven impressions that a candidate wants to make in an interview:

1. You are a true intellectual, who is a thoughtful and careful thinker.
2. You have a coherent scholarly agenda and a vision for where you see yourself as a scholar within the next five years.
3. You are articulate and enthusiastic about ideas, and you will be able to teach a class effectively.
4. You are creative and interesting, and you can generate new ideas rather than just rehash existing ones.
5. You are friendly and pleasant to be around.
6. You are confident about yourself and your work, yet not arrogant.
7. You are enthusiastic about being at the school you're interviewing with, and you will be happy living in the place where the school is located.[6]

The questions the committee will ask to try to discover these things about you, more than likely, will include the following:

"So, tell us why you want to leave private practice and come teach?"

You *must* have an answer for this. Write one down and memorize it if you have to. Nothing will sink a candidate's chances quicker than flubbing this one. You should especially avoid any answer that smacks of your looking for an easier gig than private practice. As we tried to show in chapter 1, professors may not be billing 2,400 hours a year, but it's not a cakewalk.

Acceptable answers center around two things: (1) love of the law and of research (don't overdo this with schools that also pride themselves on teaching) and (2) the difference that a professor or group of professors made to you that made you think teaching was your calling. The second is particularly effective, since it plays to professors' self-images as molders of young minds.

"Tell us a little bit about your research agenda" or *"I read your article and had a couple of questions. . . ."*

---

5. There is a standard conference-style chair sitting outside each interview suite, placed there no doubt as a courtesy to the candidate who is waiting for the preceding interview to finish. One of us (we decline to identify who) categorically refused to sit in these chairs, preferring to pace or lean on the wall, as sitting in the little chair with one's hands folded in one's lap seemed to give the impression that one had been sent into the hallway as a "time out" for bad behavior. This ridiculous mental exercise is probably an indication of the confidence-numbing impact the series of interviews can have on even the most ebullient personality. It's also probably best to avoid warm-up or loosening-up exercises in the hallway (running in place a la *Chariots of Fire* or banging one's head against the wall like a football player), as who knows who will see you, and you may disturb the ongoing interview.

6. Daniel J. Solove, *Law Teaching Interview Advice*, CONCURRING OPINIONS (Oct. 17, 2005), http://www.concurringopinions.com/archives/2005/10/law_teaching_in.html. Dan explained each of these further, and the explanations are worth reading also.

The bulk of the questioning will likely be about your scholarship, past, present, or future. Committees will often have a self-appointed scholarship czar who has slogged through all the interviewees' writings and may ask you one or two hard questions to see how you handle them. Remember: You know your writing better than anyone. If you get confused or flustered, play for time. Try restating the question: "If I understand your question, you want to know whether I . . . Is that an accurate characterization?" Or simply say, "That's a good point," and steer the conversation in another direction. (There's a fine line, of course, between playing for time and stalling or being nonresponsive. If the question is truly something you've not thought of, best admit that and move on.) You might also keep in mind that some questions are not really about your scholarship; rather, they are an opportunity for the questioners to look smart or demonstrate their expertise to their colleagues.

As to future research, it is surprising how many candidates have little to say here—or, rather, how little they have to say of any substance. Bad answers tend to be vague ("I'm interested in writing on bankruptcy and social justice.") or grandiose ("I have a book planned that will show that the Framers of the Constitution were actually Agrarian Socialists."). Good answers are specific and thought through. Ideally, they build on your earlier work, expanding it. ("In my previous article(s), I looked at _____. I have two more articles planned. The first will . . .") Your enthusiasm for your topic should be infectious—even for committee members who know nothing about the area in which you're writing.

Think about writing out your research agenda. This is something concrete that you can provide to the committee in advance, but even the exercise of creating it helps you react to this question. The more you've reflected on what you have written and where to go next, the easier this part of the interview will be, and frankly, the easier it will be to continue to write once you have a job.

In addition to a research agenda, practice your "elevator speech," basically a sentence or two that encapsulates your teaching and scholarship interests. Something like, "My teaching and scholarship interests are in constitutional law; specifically how the lower courts interpret and implement Supreme Court decisions when those decisions send few or no clear doctrinal signals." Again, thinking about that before interviews can get you ready to begin a conversation with the committee without the awkward windup in which candidates sometimes engage before hitting a conversational stride.

"What might you give as a job talk, were we to invite you back?"

As we will explain in chapter 4, the job talk is the presentation you will make to the faculty during your campus visit. If you've been asked about where your scholarship is headed, then you've likely answered this question. If not, now's your chance. It's best to select something that you have been working on for some time, and which you may have even submitted to law reviews, rather than a brand new work in progress, if possible.

"What would your ideal course package look like?"

Be honest. Say exactly what your "ideal" would be. Sometimes committees—mindful of requests made by the associate dean who plans the schedule or by faculty who want to shed a particular course—will probe to see how many needs you potentially fill. Resist the temptation to say "Whatever you want me to teach," especially if you're really interested in the school. Repeat what you put on the FAR, perhaps following up with the question, "Did you have a particular need other than the ones listed in the Job Bulletin?" If you are a Civil Procedure, Administrative Law, Legislation candidate and they ask you about your interest in teaching Sales, a simple "I really don't feel qualified to take that on" will do. On the other hand, if it's something you *would* consider, say that, too.

Be ready for the follow-up question about why you selected those courses, how they fit together, and how they fit within your research agenda. Sometimes the relationship will be relatively obvious, like teaching Civil Procedure and Complex Litigation, with a research interest in class actions. Sometimes, however, it will not be so obvious, like teaching Property and Civil Rights, with a research interest in federal courts. Being able to articulate the relationship demonstrates that you have thought quite a bit about both teaching and scholarship, which bodes well for future success at both.

"What questions do you have for us?"

This question represents another potential pitfall for interviewees. You would be surprised at how many candidates sort of phone their interviews in. You get the sense they have perhaps lost track of *which* school they are interviewing with (or details about the school, like what city it's in), like the road-weary singer who comes on in Kansas City bellowing, "Hello, Cleveland!" Committees don't like to feel as if the interviewee regards them as representatives of Generic Third-Tier Law School No. 2. You should have done your due diligence on the school, either using information they send or by doing your own research on the Web, and by learning a bit about the school from other sources. If so, then you shouldn't have any trouble coming up with questions about the school when the time comes.

While you probably will have questions that you will ask all schools, you should use the information you have acquired about the particular school to ask one or two school-specific questions, to indicate your familiarity with the school and its program. This is especially important if it is a school in which you are really interested.

Good questions for *you* to ask schools include the following:

> Does the school have a formal mentoring program for new faculty; if so, how does it work?
> Is there a formal pretenure process for newly hired faculty to receive feedback on their teaching and scholarship?
> What does the law school do to support faculty scholarship?
> Where does the law school see itself in five or ten years?
> What are the sizes of the classes and sections that I would be teaching?
> What is the course load? Are there opportunities to teach seminars/bank classes/receive light loads prior to tenure or during the first year?
> What sorts of committee responsibilities do new hires have?
> What is the law school's relationship with the university like? Are there opportunities to work with scholars in other fields?

> What's the best thing about your law school?
> What's the biggest challenge facing the law school faculty?

Keeping Time

Particularly if you have numerous interviews scheduled closely together, you must keep track of your time. Well-organized committees will have someone who is keeping a close watch on the clock, but, awkward as it is, you might have cut an interview short in order to make it to your next interview. Do this as gracefully as possible. If the interview has gone very well, you might say something like, "I hate to do this, since I'm enjoying our conversation, but I have to get to the next interview. Would it be possible to get together later to continue our discussion?" With luck, other candidates showing up for *their* interview will keep things moving. If at all possible, avoid scheduling back-to-back interviews. Keep a half-hour block of time to avoid running late and to give yourself some time to transition from one school to the next.

After the Interview

Assuming that you aren't rushing to your next interview, you should take a minute to jot down your thoughts while they are fresh. Did you feel it went well? Did you promise to send the committee a draft of your latest piece? Was there something or someone that made a particular impression, or that you are going to follow up on? Did you remember a question that you forgot to ask? These are things that you will likely forget if you don't make yourself a note. While it is not necessary to create huge databases for each interview, using a notebook to record things you learn in the interview and to jot reminders to yourself is a good idea and will prevent things from falling through the cracks.

The fact that everyone—hiring committees and candidates alike—is thrown together in the same hotel can create some potentially awkward moments. For candidates, we think the rule of thumb is this: If you see members of committees, say, sitting down having a drink at the end of the day and you want to say hello and remind them who you are, do that *quickly*. Then leave them alone. They are as tired and worn out as you are, and may be trying to collect their own thoughts on the candidates they saw that day.

There are two exceptions to this rule. The first involves the big reception for both candidates and committees. If committee members are there, they are there to schmooze with candidates, so schmooze away. The second exception is if you are invited to sit down. It may be that the committee is anxious to make a good impression on you. In that case—even if you're not as interested—you should have a seat and continue the discussion, at least for a decent interval. Of course, you can always avoid awkward interactions by confining yourself to your room and ordering room service, but remember: This is about selling yourself.

After the conference is over, write a note—we're a little old-fashioned, so "write" here doesn't mean "e-mail"—to the hiring chair of all the schools you visited thanking them for the opportunity to interview with them. For the schools in which you are truly interested, write each member of the committee thanking them, then go ahead and ask for the opportunity to do a campus visit. At least that will leave no doubt about your interest.

Then you wait. In some cases, your wait will not be long. Frequently, committees will meet immediately after their last interview and make calls at least to a few favorite interviewees on Saturday evening or Sunday. In other cases, schools may have to get some sort of official (usually university-level) approval to bring candidates to campus, so there may be a delay of a week or more. So, do not panic if you don't hear from anyone on Saturday or Sunday.

Probably the hardest thing to do is *not* to call or write the schools in which you are interested asking for updates. The process is not unlike dating. You want to seem interested, but not *too* interested—and you certainly don't want to seem desperate or needy. The best advice we have is this: When in doubt, *don't*. The committee knows where you can be contacted, and will get in touch with you if further conversations are warranted. Except for the thank-you note, it is your turn to wait for them.

The only exception to this rule is if things begin to move quickly with other opportunities and you have not heard from one or more schools you prefer. Then, on the theory that nothing makes you popular like being popular, you should let them know what's going on, express continued interest, and ask whether it would be possible for you to hear from them sooner rather than later on the possibility of a callback.

One final note. Waiting on callbacks is torture. It is full of wishful thinking, self-deception, rationalization, and rueful recollection. While a complete disaster is usually apparent at the time, assume nothing positive is correlated to a callback. Do not mistake vigorous interaction, smiles and nods, or a detailed discussion of how well your qualifications fit the school's needs for anything other than what they are. Moreover, "radio silence" is rarely good. Committees don't usually get back to you to say you are out of the process, and you can assume any snail mail letter with the school's address on it is a message to that effect. In many cases of continued silence, you missed the first cut of callbacks, but the committee doesn't want to let you go in case it needs to go to the B team, and it doesn't want to tell you that you are on the B team, even though it's clear that if you don't get called in the first couple of weeks after the FRC, you are either out of the game or on the B team.

PRECONFERENCE INTERVIEWS

A recent development in the world of law school hiring has been the willingness of certain schools to conduct interviews and extend offers *before* the AALS conference. In some cases, schools will extend offers that expire if not accepted before the conference begins ("exploding offers"). It is not clear how widespread this is becoming, or even if it can be described fairly as a trend. You should be aware of the phenomenon, and think over how you might handle that situation, should it arise.

First, it is important to distinguish between preconference *screening interviews*, which approximate the thirty-minute interview in Washington, and the full-scale interview of candidates and extension of offers. The former often occur when schools are filling a large number of vacancies, or are located near a large number of candidates. For example, schools in New York and New Jersey may invite candidates living close by for a short interview with the hiring committee. These interviews may last a little longer than usual—you may get a tour of the building, for example—but do not usually involve your giving a job talk. The committee will likely wait until they completed interviews in Washington before deciding whom to ask back for an on-campus visit.

This is a common practice, and one that you might welcome. For one thing, it gives you a little practice out of the hurly-burly of the actual conference. The committee will likely be fresher as well. Moreover, it frees up your schedule for the conference, allowing you either to interview more schools or to space out the interviews you do have.

The emerging practice we want to make you aware of may begin with a short interview, either in person or over the phone; the difference is that following that interview, you may be invited to visit the campus, give the job talk, meet with the entire faculty, and so on, before ever going to Washington. In some cases, offers will be extended prior to the conference and, as mentioned, may expire once the conference begins.

This practice is controversial, and is the subject of AALS discussion about whether it needs to be regulated or eliminated. Some schools that have done it in the past defend it, especially when attempting to fill an unusual number of vacancies. Critics of the practice note that it undermines the efficiency of the AALS process itself and might severely undermine the conference if it becomes widespread. It puts tremendous pressure on candidates, who, hearing how scarce jobs are, might feel obligated to take the bird in the hand, ending up at a school that might not be the best fit. It could also disadvantage schools that are relatively difficult to travel to. It is also an enormous gamble for schools. Hiring committees might have a difficult time persuading their colleagues that several candidates are better than anyone else they might interview in Washington, based only on a review of all candidates' paper records. Schools may also rightly worry that making exploding offers and pressuring candidates may not put their own school in the best light. If you coerce someone into accepting your offer, they may join your faculty, especially if they are risk averse, but could resent the way in which the offer was extended.

Because schools are somewhat cagey about advertising that this is the way they operate, it is difficult to know whether this is the wave of the future, or just an attempt by a few schools to gain a competitive advantage. Our guess is the latter; if it becomes widespread, we expect complaints to multiply and for the AALS to step in to curb abuses, like ending offers that expire at the beginning of the hiring conference (although one of us practiced antitrust law and would wonder about the legality of such a restriction).

Conference Timeline

February–March
> Spring law review submissions season—submit any completed drafts to law reviews.
> Contact those whom you are going to ask to be listed as references.
> Begin work on possible subjects for "job talks" to be given at callback interviews.

July
> Update and proofread resume.
> Have someone review both the FAR form and CV prior to submission.
> Register with the AALS; upload FAR form and CV.

August
> Submit job talk to law reviews.
> Mail letters to hiring committee chairs of schools advertising in the Job Bulletin.
> Reserve room at the AALS.

September
> Schedule D.C. interviews with schools that have contacted you.
> Review the Job Bulletin for new ads and contact those schools.

September–October
> Schedule mock interviews.
> Practice mock job talks.

October–November
> AALS Hiring Conference.
> Follow up with schools via thank-you letters.
> Schedule callback interviews.

The On-Campus Interview

Like the proverbial ice-cream eating contest whose reward is more ice cream, the reward for succeeding at the AALS Faculty Recruitment Conference is— you guessed it!—*more* interviewing. As early as the evening of the first day of the conference, but usually later, you'll receive invitations to travel to the campus of the interested law school. There you will do two things that we cover in this chapter: interview with more people, both at the law school and, perhaps, at the host university; and give the dreaded "job talk." This callback is an opportunity for both you and the faculty to get to know one another better.

Earlier we mentioned that joining a faculty is sort of like joining a family. If the recruiting conference is like dating, the callback is like meeting the parents (and the extended family, including the crazy uncle). Therefore, this chapter will include some archetypical (which sounds better than "stereotypical") law schools and faculty members you are likely to encounter. Among other things, you should think hard about two questions. Is this the *type* of law school at which I could be happy? Are these the *type* of people I wouldn't mind seeing every day of my working career? Resist the desire to choose a school based on rankings or perceived prestige. That is not a very good reason for students to choose a law school for three years. It is an exceptionally bad basis for your choice of where to spend potentially your entire career.

At the same time, though, you probably should not accept a callback at a school from which you are truly sure you would not accept an offer. If you accept only as a way to leverage an offer from another school, and this gets out, you will have done serious damage to your reputation. The teaching community is surprisingly small. On the other hand, if there is any chance you would accept, and you have not too many scheduled, you should go. Often seeing a school first-hand, meeting the people there, and getting a glimpse of the community makes you reevaluate your initial impressions.

THE LOGISTICS OF THE CALLBACK

It sounds straightforward. You (and, depending on the number of positions to be filled, three or four others at different times) will travel to the law school, at its expense, for at least a daylong round of interviews. Ordinarily, you will be taken to dinner either the night before or as a conclusion to your day of interviews (occasionally both). You will very likely be taken to breakfast the morning of the interview day. During your stay, you will undoubtedly see some of the members of the appointments committee, but they will tend to recede into the background as you spend time with the rest of the faculty. At some point during the day—at most places it occurs at noon—you will give your job talk, discussed more below, and answer questions about it. If the law school is part of a university, you may meet with the provost of the university; there is usually a campus tour; and, at the end of the day, you have an exit interview with the dean, who will usually ask if you have any final questions and may indicate the time frame in which you might expect to hear something from the school.

For this to go as smoothly as we've described above, however, you need both a committee that has its act together—which you don't have much control over—and *you* need to make sure that you prepare even more than you did for the AALS recruiting conference.

Pre-Callback Preparation

As soon as possible, look over the members of the faculty. Is there anyone there who writes in your area? Have you cited them? Have they cited you? If the answer to any of those questions is "yes," you should start by skimming their articles—as well as your own. Those will likely be the faculty members who will be looked to by their colleagues to pass judgment on your scholarship and comment on your potential as a scholar. You want to walk away from your visit with those folks as your allies.

Most schools will give you a schedule in advance, giving you times of meetings and names of persons with whom you'll be interviewing. But know that the schedule may change, and faculty may sit in at the last minute. The more you know about the faculty as a whole, the easier it will be to make it through those interviews where everyone seems to be waiting for you to be brilliant. As we'll discuss below, preparation means coming armed with questions for them, too.

Before you visit, look at the faculty bios on the school's Web site. If you know the names of the faculty members that you will speak with, print their bios and pictures. You might make notes about their work to help you remember who they are or to think of questions for them. You might want to print out other faculty bios as well, particularly of those who write or teach in your area. Sometimes faculty Web pages are not entirely up-to-date. If you are feeling extremely ambitious, you might look up the faculty in the AALS Directory of Law Teachers, which most law school libraries and faculty members have a copy of. That gets updated every year with the subjects faculty members have taught most recently.

During your visit, you will have a "shepherd,"[1] a faculty contact, often but not always the head of the hiring committee. That shepherd will be your primary contact and can be a valuable resource to find out more about the process and the faculty. Don't be afraid to ask questions to get some advance understanding of the faculty you will be meeting and about what kind of job talk you should present. This person will likely be a strong supporter of your candidacy, so take advantage of that. On the one hand, you don't want to ask any sensitive questions, but if you feel comfortable and have established a rapport, it is a good idea to ask, "Is there anything I should look out for?" or some similar question designed to ask for help. Faculty members will often spill their guts at this point, and much can be gleaned about the school itself, and the best approach to interviewing.

Finally, you should find as much information as you can about the university, as well as the city or town and state in which it is located. (If the law school or university materials don't have enough information for you, the local chamber of commerce will inundate you with information of all kinds. Many municipalities have Web sites of varying quality that could be helpful as well.) Being able to talk knowledgeably about the university and the area and ask intelligent questions denotes a level of preparation that you want to convey to schools in which you have genuine interest. It also shows that you are genuinely interested in discovering whether you would enjoy living there.

Preparing for your callbacks is both exciting and nerve-wracking. You might think about channeling that nervous energy into making sure you are well organized. Instead of printing out a bunch of material and cramming it into folders and expandable files, consider making binders for each school you'll visit. These could be organized in different ways; see the box for suggested information to include. This may seem like organizational overkill, but if you have even a handful of callbacks, the schools, their faculty, and the interviews will tend to run together quickly.

Scheduling the Time Off

Scheduling can be a tricky issue if you're currently employed and if you end up with multiple callbacks. Ultimately, only you can make the decision whether to travel clandestinely to callbacks or disclose what you're doing to your employer. But before you assume that disclosure would be foolish, especially if you don't end up getting a job, consider the experience of a number of people we know who, after much agonizing, decided that it was only fair to disclose to their firm that they were a candidate and would have to take some time for callbacks. To their surprise, firms often permitted them to use firm

---

1. Thanks to Debra Cohen for this term. Deb has been to the Faculty Recruitment Conference every year since 1993 as a candidate, recruiter, and for quite some time, resource for candidates. Her article, *Matchmaker, Matchmaker, Make Me a Match* (Sept. 2006), http://ssrn.com/abstract=931995, is an excellent resource for candidates.

Suggested Table of Contents for On-Campus Binder

1. Schedule
2. General information about law school, university, and location
3. Faculty biographies, including
    a. Notes on classes taught
    b. Copies of scholarship in your area that you have cited or that cited you
    c. Faculty-specific questions
4. General questions for faculty and students
5. Notes for job talk, including handouts and hard copies of visual aides
6. A copy of your job talk paper
7. Space for post-visit impressions

Also Remember

Copies of CV

Extra reprints of publications

resources and devote time to preparing for the interviews. So enthusiastic was the response for some of our friends that partners sent the word out to leave them alone while they prepared. This response may be atypical in an era of enormous associate salaries that *someone* has to pay for, but we suspect that the partners were enjoying living vicariously a little through their faculty candidates. When one of us (Denning) left practice for an LL.M. program, nearly every partner he told at his firm expressed enthusiasm and admiration—and most noted, wistfully, how much they always wanted to teach or write.

Traveling

Callbacks are stressful events. Try to arrange things so as to minimize the number of additional things that cause you anxious moments during your visit. This visit is your second (and last) chance to stand out, so you want to be well rested, mentally alert, and focused on the task at hand. Unless the distance is such that driving would take *less* time, fly or take the train to your callback. Moreover, try to schedule your travel so you arrive the afternoon or evening before the next day's interviews. Not only will that give you an opportunity to get a good night's sleep, but also if you experience travel delays (always possible around the year-end holidays), they can be resolved without scotching the whole interview, as might happen if you tried to travel in and out on the same day.

Since delays happen, be sure that you have the cell phone number of someone on the committee whom you can contact if you need to; conversely, make sure that committee members have a number where *you* can be reached if your ride is going to be late, or if there are other last-minute changes in plans. Especially if you are flying, you might consider carrying on essentials that could get you through the next day if your luggage is lost. If you have audiovisual materials for your job talk, like a PowerPoint presentation, you might consider both carrying it on a portable hard drive *and* e-mailing it to someone at the school you're visiting, so there will be multiple copies available just in case. Be sure, too, that you can deliver a good presentation without those materials if, for some reason, you can't make them work once you get there.

THE VISIT

In thinking about making a good impression in your interviews and with your job talk, it is easy to overlook another important aspect of the visit—does the school appeal to *you*? Sometimes it is so easy to forget that if the hiring committee has invited you back for a visit at the school's expense, they are as eager to make a good impression on you as you are on them. Or they should be. If not, that should tell you something about the school. During the hurly-burly of the visit, don't forget that you have to be alert and observant for little clues about what it would be like to work there every day for several years. Does the building look well-maintained, even if it's a little dated? Do students and staff seem happy? Do faculty seem at ease with one another? Since the school will be putting on its best face for your visit, you'll likely have to rely on subtle clues for answers to these questions.

But we're getting a little ahead of ourselves. You might begin by asking yourself what *kind* of law school you are visiting. "Is there more than one kind of law school?" you might be asking. The short answer is "yes." How the law school faculty perceives its law school may tell you a great deal about what it would be like to work there. Finding a match between the type of law school in which you would like to teach and the self-perception of a particular school is essential to a good match for both. In addition to purely descriptive categories like accredited versus unaccredited, profit versus not-for-profit, public versus private, and religiously affiliated versus secular, we think that most law schools can be characterized as follows: (1) elite; (2) "elitistic"; (3) up-and-coming; (4) transitional; or (5) practice-focused. The usual disclaimer—that these represent points along a continuum instead of hermetically sealed categories—applies with particular force to the overbroad generalizations we offer below.

1. *Elite.* These are the top law schools, which employ graduates of other elite law schools. In many ways, elite law school hiring is sui generis; many hire either only laterally, or according to a plan that differs substantially from the one that we've described here. In a nutshell, their

new faculty members are expected not simply to publish, but to publish cutting-edge, paradigm-shifting legal scholarship in the nation's top law journals. Many have already done so before being hired. There is usually a corresponding lessened emphasis on teaching effectiveness, however measured. If an elite law school is courting you, congratulations! But as with any decision, be sure the environment is one in which you feel comfortable. Just because a school is elite doesn't mean it's necessarily the best place to work for everyone. The upside is that places like this are vibrant intellectual atmospheres with numerous outside speakers, colloquia, symposia and the like. You'll also get many chances to present your work before other audiences. Additionally, you will have access to all of the resources that excellent research institutions can provide. And your students will likely be intellectually engaged and interested in the same kinds of things you are. Potential downsides might include a difficult road to tenure, the stress of producing legal scholarship that meets expectations, possible isolation that can result from colleagues so immersed in their own work that they don't have time to provide useful input for yours, and the kind of faculty politics that can result from a collection of brilliant minds, strong wills, and no shortage of, ahem, healthy egos.

2. *Elitistic.* We made this term up. We learned in Western Civilization that "Hellenic" described Greek civilization, while "Hellenistic" described "Greek-like" civilizations, like the Macedonians. Similarly, there are a number of law schools that, while not technically "elite," certainly style themselves as "elite-like." In some cases, the expectations may be higher here than at actual elite schools, depending on how much pressure there is to demonstrate that the law school is as good as (or better than) the schools considered elite by arbiters of such things (like *U.S. News & World Report*). Prepare for a minimum of small talk in faculty interviews and don't expect polite applause at the conclusion of your job talk. Expect people to have read your articles, listen attentively, and question rigorously your talk. The upsides to this kind of environment in terms of the intellectual atmosphere and resources for scholarship are similar to those at elite schools with the added benefit that your colleagues may be engaged in their scholarship, but will likely be interested in yours as well! Students, too, are often eager to prove their intellectual mettle—to show that the elite law schools that rejected them really missed out. Potential downsides are similar to those at elite law schools and may include a potentially difficult road to tenure, the stress of producing legal scholarship that meets expectations, less of an assumption by outsiders that you are a brilliant scholar, and perhaps an unhealthy competition among junior faculty as a result. Even without those, the pressure to move up in the rankings year after year can be demoralizing by itself.

3. *Up-and-coming.* An up-and-coming law school is usually a former "transitional" law school (described below) that aspires to be elitistic. It will probably share many characteristics of the elitistic law school. There will probably be an energetic dean who has thrown the weight of his or her

office behind scholarly production. There might be a large number of new faculty hired specifically to carry out the dean's vision. There may be some of the same intellectual energy and excitement among the faculty. What sets up-and-coming law schools from elitistic ones is that more often than not, the student body may not be of the same quality, overall, as the faculty. This can produce some tensions, with faculty becoming dissatisfied at a perceived lack of intellectual curiosity among the students, and students dissatisfied at perceived lack of interest in training them to be practicing lawyers as opposed to panelists at scholarly symposia. Faculty politics may also present greater conflict with strongly held views on how the school can most effectively achieve elitistic status.

4. *Transitional.* These law schools are schools that had primarily seen their mission as training lawyers for the practice of law, but that have begun to adjust that mission to include the recruitment of faculty that will also produce scholarship. It may be that a core group of faculty has agitated for an alteration in focus; perhaps a new dean has made increased productivity a goal of the school. However it happens, transitional schools will be hiring faculty who show scholarly promise, and will begin rewarding productivity. But transitional schools will also have a contingent of faculty who may have a vested interest in maintaining the vocational focus of the school. Similarly, the school's students may become alienated from the school's shift if they perceive it as coming at the expense of a "real world" legal education. Both of these can produce tensions within the law school that can be difficult to navigate. If a group of faculty (usually older and politically powerful) decides to dig in its heels and resist the transformation, everything from curricular reforms to hiring to promotion and tenure decisions can become a fight. However, not all transitions are contentious. Much depends on the manner in which the reorientation from teaching alone to teaching plus scholarship is carried out.

5. *Practice-focused.* We would guess that *U.S. News & World Report*'s annual rankings have forced most law schools to embrace scholarship to some degree, given the weight assigned to peer evaluations by the survey. Nevertheless, a significant number of schools still regard training students for the practice of law as their primary mission. They will tend to favor applicants with significant practice experience, will tend to offer bread-and-butter courses as opposed to esoteric or exotic seminars, and may not view highly theoretical legal scholarship as the highest and best use of a professor's nonteaching time. This type of school might be an excellent fit for someone who would like to teach, but who is less interested in the type of legal scholarship valued by the academy at large (as opposed to practitioner-oriented articles and treatises, or teaching materials). It will be less appealing to someone who has an ambitious scholarly agenda and who wants to be at a place where ideas are discussed and debated, drafts exchanged, and with speakers and colloquia.

You will likely know in advance what type of school you are visiting. Most law schools either regard themselves as up-and-coming or transitional, and if you have graduated with a non-elite J.D. and an elite LL.M. these are likely the schools with which you will be interviewing. You should consider—at a school that is really making a push toward more and better faculty scholarship—whether the pressure will motivate or unnerve you. Do you feel that competition among younger faculty is unhealthy or might it seem unhealthy as it exists at a particular institution? By the same token, do you want to be the first junior faculty member at a law school that is trying to make some transition to the world of publishing and legal scholarship? Do you sense that there is opposition to that transition? To answer these questions, you are going to have to be observant during your campus visit.

Meet the Faculty

While you've already met the members of the appointments committee, it shouldn't come as any surprise that the committee is often a law school's attempt to put its very best foot forward at the hiring conference. You may meet an entirely different set of people when you visit with the rest of the faculty. If you've never been part of a faculty generally, or a law faculty in particular, you might think that our generalizations here are too sweeping to be of much use. But think about the professors at your own law school; you're bound to recognize some of these archetypes.

> *The Old Guard.* Just about every school we know of has a set of gray eminences that are both the keepers of the school's institutional memory and are often politically quite powerful. They are treated with respect, sometimes bordering on reverence, and, if you want to teach at that school, you would be wise to do the same. At their best, members of the old guard are reasonable, thoughtful, slow to anger or excite, and serve as the dean's counselors. Even if they are not productive scholars, they have taught generations of students, are quite well known, and often quite popular with alums. They often are a source of great comfort to young faculty, whom they mentor and advise selflessly. At their worst, however, these folks can be dinosaurs: resistant to change, suspicious of innovation, and fiercely protective of their prerogatives and territory. They may resent newer faculty—particularly those who teach in their area, and might even go so far as to attempt to sabotage them, denigrating their teaching and scholarship to faculty and students alike. They may befriend new faculty only to secure some advantage, and friendship may come with the price of expected support for the older faculty's hobbyhorses.

> *The Young Stars.* These faculty members reside at the other end of the spectrum: recent hires who have joined the faculty and become instant successes. They have taught brilliantly, been prolific scholars, and enjoy influence as a result. Particularly at up-and-coming or transitional schools, these folks will tend to be your natural allies—for the most part. If tenured, they will be making a push to hire more like them; if not, they will still be arguing as much as they can for continuing to consider productivity and scholarly promise in hiring decisions. They will usually

offer an honest (if circumspect) account of life as a young professor on the faculty, and will often help explain to you the lay of the land at the school. There is a chance that these young stars will also be your toughest critics. Eager to prove their mettle, they may be aggressive in questioning you during your job talk or during the interviews. Don't take it personally, but do be wary if you teach in the same or similar areas. Even young stars, particularly untenured ones, can be insecure about their place on the faculty and within the school. They may not relish having to share the spotlight with *another* young star!

> *The Workhorses.* The old 80/20 rule of organizations holds that 80 percent of the work in an organization is done by 20 percent of the people in that group. The same rule generally applies to faculties as well. (The other 80/20 rule is that 80 percent of any organization thinks it ranks in that 20 percent. That's probably true of faculties, but a topic for a different book.) Every faculty has a group of professors who are good teachers, who sign up for all the working committees, who attend alumni functions, and who serve as advisors to student organizations and coach the moot court teams. Some of these faculty members will have been productive scholars; many might not have written anything in a while. Often they will be most interested in ascertaining what kind of *colleague* you would be. Would you be willing to do your share of work, or would you be a prima donna, constantly demanding special favors and contributing little in return? Many probably spent their entire careers at the law school and look with distrust on someone they perceive to be using the law school as a stepping stone.

> *The Malcontents.* With luck, those who are alienated from the rest of the faculty or otherwise disaffected will not participate much in the hiring process. If not, these faculty are easy to spot by their sarcastic tone, open (or barely veiled) contempt for colleagues and students, and general negative attitude about the school and everyone in it. Sometimes the malcontents will form tight knots and will corner interviewees to give them a hard time. Observant hiring chairs will know who they are and try to keep that from happening, but it does occasionally. Be on guard with these folks and try to give them as little ammunition as possible to deploy against you. While often simply ignored by others on the faculty, they can sometimes still find enough support to make mischief.

> *The Wraiths.* There's a good chance that you will not see these folks at all—their colleagues may not even see them that much. These are faculty that, if not for the fact that they managed to turn in exams every year, people might not realize were even on the faculty. Other than teaching class and attending the occasional faculty meeting, these folks are never present in the law school. They seem to materialize, teach, then vanish into the ether—and not because their spare time is spent churning out scholarship either. Wraiths may be, but are not necessarily, malcontents. In other cases, family circumstances, or outside interests, like consulting, occupy their nonteaching time.

The Interviews

The actual arrangement of the interviews varies from school to school. Some schools have a series of one-on-one interviews, where the candidate moves from office to office. Sometimes the candidate stays in the same room, and groups of two or three faculty members at a time come in. Some schools use a mix of both, as well as a "drop in" session to which anyone is welcome. The interviews usually take place both before and after your job talk. These can range from polite chats where it is obvious that the person conducting the interview has just barely glanced over your CV to full-contact interviews where you are interrogated on everything from your scholarship to your teaching style to current legal controversies. Since the interviews can be composed of faculty from each of the categories described above, the results can be "interesting," which is a euphemism for "extremely unsettling." Remember, though, that every faculty has some irrepressible eccentrics; don't necessarily judge the school based on cranky or even inappropriate comments from a single member. Try to roll with it, and know that it will probably last only about twenty more minutes. It helps if you are prepared to ask questions that will get others talking. This can be difficult at the end of the day when, in truth, you've probably had a good number of your questions answered. Still, there are a few that you ought to hold in reserve, or ask of each person you talk with, to see how or whether different faculty members' answers differ. The following are good questions:

> What attracted you to this law school?
> What do you enjoy most about teaching here?
> Where do you think the law school needs improving?

> If the law school received a $50 million gift today, what would you want done with it?
> What are the students like here? What are their expectations of professors? What are your expectations of them?
> What do you think this law school will look like in five years?
> What is the relationship between the law school and the main university [if applicable, or "with other schools in the area" if applicable].
> Do you provide formal or informal mentoring of junior faculty?

If you get time alone with untenured faculty, you might ask about collegiality, whether there is sufficient support for and encouragement of scholarship, and whether the teaching loads are manageable. Pay particular attention to their answers: If they seem hesitant or evasive, you will want to note that.

Many times you will have an opportunity to meet with groups of students during your visit. These represent both an opportunity to gain real insight into the school and yet another pitfall for interviewees. Students are often shrewd observers of their own school and can be willing to share information that no one else will. Ask questions such as "What do you like most/ least about the law school?" "What characteristics do you admire most in the professors at this school?" "What changes would you make at the law school if you could?" That is a way both to communicate your interest in the things that are going to be most important to them, as well as eliciting information that tells you a lot about the personality of the law school itself.

Students are probably not going to want to talk much about your scholarship agenda; in fact, they may be put off by constant reference to it on your part. Sometimes students get the idea that a professor who is engaged in scholarship will have less interest in teaching, mentoring, or advising student groups. Don't forget, too, that students are involved in the interview process for a reason. The recruiting committee will solicit their views and the faculty—particularly at schools placing a high premium on teaching and student involvement—will consider those views. More than once we've seen promising candidates hurt themselves by blowing the student interviews.

The Job Talk

The "job talk" is the period during the day when you will make a presentation to the faculty about something you have either published or that you are currently writing.[2] This is the most important part of your trip, for all sorts of reasons. (For advice on writing the paper that will be your job talk, see chapter 2.) Job talks are usually—but not always—scheduled during the lunch hour or the early afternoon. It is vitally important that you prepare for this talk, giving careful thought to what you are going to talk about and how you structure your presentation. For faculty who otherwise don't meet you during the day (and there may be quite a few in that category), it will be their only impression of you. (This is particularly true where the school provides lunch to the faculty. Few things move large numbers of faculty members like the prospect of free food.) Faculty will not only be listening to the substance of your presentation, they will be watching how you present and how you handle questions—inferring from that how you might be in a classroom. Many a promising candidate has torpedoed his or her chances with a poor job talk. In some ways, it's like oral argument: The job talk alone won't get you a job, but it can lose you a job you were otherwise likely to get.

There's an important caveat here. Very little of what follows is cast in stone. There are some things we feel fairly sure can be presented as universal truths, like do *not* read your job talk, particularly from little index cards using a meek voice that can only be heard by people three feet from you, while failing to look up enough even to make eye contact with the top of the lectern. (Trust us, we've seen it happen.) Even we don't agree on many things beyond the basics. Some of us like PowerPoint; some of us hate it. (More importantly, some faculties hate PowerPoint, and that's a good thing to know!) Some of us are comfortable wandering around without notes and without a lectern; some of us need the physical support. At some point, you have to be decisive about what works for you, and go with it. On close questions about format

---

2. We have heard of schools that ask candidates to make a presentation as if they were teaching a class. This is probably not the norm. It should send a signal, however, about the relative priorities of that law school. Many candidates ended up creating some sort of ersatz "lesson" based on a recently published or in-progress work.

and technique, the best thing to do is to call your contact at the school and ask. Don't worry about sounding silly; there's enough variation that almost any question is a good one. Above all, though, stick primarily to the style you are most comfortable with. If you are technologically challenged, don't use PowerPoint even if the host faculty likes it, for example.

Choice of Topics

Most people would say the ideal topic is something you have published or substantially completed and submitted to law reviews by the time you are asked to give your job talk. If possible—and in the absence of a specific request made by the school—go with something that is finished and submitted to law reviews in the August submission season. Because that piece will likely be accepted for publication by the time of your callback, you can use that information as a talking point to start your job talk or as an excuse to contact the committee. At the very least, the job talk is not the forum for presenting a half-baked idea that you've barely begun to research.[3] You want the topic to be something that you know well enough not to be surprised by questions, and on which you can converse comfortably, even if you haven't completed all your research or reading. You don't want to be spending the weeks leading up to your job talks frantically building up your knowledge base on a topic prior to presenting it to an audience for the first time.

One of the great mentors to new professors, Professor Larry Solum at the University of Illinois, has suggested that there are several stages in the genesis of a publishable article, particularly in this era of Web-based disintermediation of scholarship on sites like SSRN. There is a point at which an idea has enough traction to be a ten- or fifteen-page thought piece, and one that you feel confident enough to put out for the public, even though it is not complete. That kind of work is good fodder for the job talk if you don't have a submitted piece.[4]

If you go with something that is less than final, be up front with your audience about the "in progress" nature of the talk. If you *are* presenting something that you've already published, be sure to *reread* your paper prior to presenting it. Not everyone will have read it—most will probably not have. Nothing, though, is more embarrassing than contradicting what you've written or not being able to answer a question about your article because it's been a while since you skimmed it.

---

3. There is actually a place for these kinds of talks by established faculty, sometimes called "brown bags." Usually, though, even when an established faculty member gives a lunch talk on something in progress, it is farther along than a few ideas scratched out on a notepad. Job talks really are in the category of lunch talks, and it's not expected that what you are saying is your final word on the subject. Again, as noted, this is subject to nuance. A really interesting theoretical concept might not have to be as far along as, say, a fruitful, but yet to be undertaken, empirical project.

4. This raises another, and broader, issue about the legal academy generally. The point of dissemination vehicles like SSRN is to allow works in progress to be circulated. The tension for many young scholars is what, indeed, may be considered too half-baked for presentation even as a thought piece.

One question that often arises: Should you send a draft of a piece that is substantially completed, but not yet finished? Our view is that you should. If you make it plain that it is a work in progress and thus might not be Bluebooked perfectly, send it on. If you advertise that you have something almost finished, but don't let members of the committee or the faculty see it, you'll raise suspicions that perhaps it isn't as far along as you're advertising, or worse, that you're not too confident about its quality.

The general rule (again, subject to many exceptions) is that your job talk should be germane to the position for which you're being considered. If you're selling yourself as a health law expert, but present a new theory of the First Amendment in your job talk, faculty will naturally wonder about the sincerity of the interest in the position. Some of us think (this is one of the exceptions to the general rule) that it's better to go with the most complete work, even if it is outside the scope of the courses you would be teaching at your callback school, especially if it is a school that does not expect faculty to write in the areas they teach. And even if it is not, a simple explanation at the beginning of your talk might assuage skeptics. It might be that you expanded a law school paper in a class you found particularly interesting. Or the paper might have grown out of an experience in practice or an issue that arose when you were clerking. Whatever the reason, be prepared to give one, lest people wonder why the commercial law candidate is talking about public international law! One additional caution here. If you do not plan to continue writing in that area, you must nonetheless embrace the questions that push your conclusions to the next step or challenge your thesis. Part of the job is being intellectually curious and a rigorous thinker. A response like, "Well, I'm not actually interested in that anymore" would be very harmful.

One of the most common mistakes job candidates make is overestimating the knowledge level of their audience. An audience of law professors will invariably be bright, and engaged by interesting ideas, but beyond the basics of the first-year courses, there's probably not a whole lot of common ground in terms of expertise. This is certainly true of specialized areas like tax or administrative law, but also don't assume that everyone in the room is a constitutional scholar, or up-to-date on the most recent trends in juvenile justice. The reason job talks are so important is that faculty talks, by their nature, are teaching sessions, in which the expert shares his or her expertise with lay people, albeit very bright lay people who may know something about fields that are contiguous with, or otherwise related to, the expert's. If you can teach the teachers, you probably can teach the students.

Format

Most job talks are around an hour. You should plan on talking for about twenty or so minutes, leaving time open for questions at the end. Err on the side of shorter rather than longer; it's much better to give a twenty-minute talk than a thirty-five-minute talk. Give careful thought to handouts or PowerPoint slides—especially if your topic is technical or involves numerous statutory provisions. If you use PowerPoint, though, remember that less is more. Reading your PowerPoint slides word for word is, in some quarters, as great a sin as reading little index cards. (And don't forget to let someone know that you'll need audiovisual support.) Even basic visual aids such as an outline will help those who have not read your article follow your presentation. Again, when in doubt, ask your host! Some faculties are known to like handouts; some faculties don't respond well to PowerPoint.

Depending on the type of school you're visiting, you might find yourself speaking the entire time or, if you have the faculty equivalent of a "hot bench," you might not get very far in your prepared remarks at all. The usual faculty approach is another good area to ask your host about. For some faculty, the job talk is a contact sport. These faculty members will be lying in wait to pounce on you with challenges, questions tangential (at best) to your point, and bizarre hypotheticals. It is important that you not allow yourself to be rattled, to say nothing of becoming defensive. On the other hand, you might end up doing all the talking, and get little more than a few desultory questions at the end. This doesn't mean that your talk didn't go well. It might simply reflect the fact that no one else in the room knew much about the subject of your talk! It might also mean that you blew them away with your concise, illuminating presentation.

A couple of points to remember. Again, ask your host about the format. If you are expecting folks to hold all questions until the end, you might be thrown by someone interrupting to ask a question and find it hard to retrieve the thread of your comments. Inviting folks to ask questions as they occur not only makes you seem relaxed and confident, it might actually spark a lively dialogue with the faculty. Second, don't read to the faculty. Remember that this will be used as a proxy for likely classroom performance. If you're dull in the job talk, faculty might come away convinced you'd be dull in the classroom, too. You definitely don't want to leave *that* impression.

A Taxonomy of Likely Questions and Questioners

Having attended a number of workshops and job talks, we know that there are an infinite number of questions that could be asked. In fact, it never fails to surprise us that while different presentations yield some of the same questions, there are always new ones. Still, most questions, and many questioners, fall into a few categories. We'll lay out some of the problematic ones here and suggest ways to address them.

Some difficult questions can be avoided by explaining at the outset the parameters of the research and giving a logical explanation for the reason you chose those parameters. This introduction will give your audience an understanding that you made principled decisions about your research rather than letting them assume that you missed something. You also might acknowledge any weakness in your paper as part of your talk, explaining why it exists. That is widely known as the "to be sure" section of a presentation, in which you acknowledge and attempt to preempt possible objections.

There are three other things to remember about questions and questioners generally. First, recall that many questions come from people wishing to demonstrate their own knowledge and expertise to their own faculty (or, sometimes, we think cynically, to themselves if they see themselves as the master of a particular area). Second, no matter how pointed the questioning, remember the wisdom of *The Godfather*: "It's not personal, it's business." Interviews and job talks are as good a time as any for you to separate criticism of your work from criticism of you as a person. This may be hard to believe, but most law faculties (compared to some of the other more notorious disciplines) are generally soft touches about presentations, particularly in the job talk setting. (There are some well-known exceptions, but if you are giving a talk at one of those schools, you probably already know that.) Our sense is that most faculty members hope to hear a great talk and want you to succeed. Third, sometimes what you take as aggression isn't aggression at all, but just the questioner's manner. The thing to keep in mind during the job talk, therefore, is to welcome the questioning and at least seem interested and enthused about giving a thoughtful answer.

Never get so emotionally invested in your ideas that you conflate probing questions with a personal attack. Easier said than done, we know, but you have to at least affect distance from your work during job talks. It's hard to get this far and not be a little Type-A defensive (trust us, we all are), but do your best not to be. Not only will a defensive or hostile response to questions likely provoke more questions, much like blood in the water can ignite a feeding frenzy among sharks, but it will probably lead even your ardent champions on the faculty to abandon you. If anyone should be able to give you candid assessments of your scholarship, it should be members of your own faculty. Many will extrapolate from your inability or unwillingness to hear criticism of your scholarship a telltale arrogance or rigidity that would make you an undesirable colleague.

The Frontal Assault

This is the question that we probably fear the most, but get relatively rarely, the question that calls into question everything you have said. Many times this one is asked by someone who has strong, deeply held beliefs about the subject or your approach, or else by someone who feels he or she has something to prove to the rest of the faculty.

It's easy to panic or get defensive, neither of which is in your interest. Take a deep breath and a moment to think before you answer this, and keep in mind that the rest of your audience likely realizes what this questioner is doing. One strategy you might use is to restate the question in a calm tone to ask whether you understand it correctly, to defuse any hostility in the speaker's tone, and to give yourself a minute to think. Then fall back on your research or on other voices in your field. Don't be afraid to acknowledge that approaches to legal questions may be diametrically opposed or irreconcilably conflicted. You can quite explicitly agree to disagree on fundamental points that are contested.

Another strategy is to remember that part of what the faculty is judging is your ability to teach. Be a teacher by being a learner. Start a dialogue.

"Obviously you know a lot about this area and have a strong view. Help me understand it." "Explain to me the difference between your position and mine." "Do you think there is a middle ground?"

The Non Sequitur

You may have just given a brilliant explanation of a complicated issue in transactional law, most of the room is nodding, you've answered a few questions pushing you slightly on some of your points when someone in the back of the room asks, "What about the Seventh Amendment right to a jury trial here?" Your immediate thought may be to wonder whether the faculty member was even in the room for your talk, or to panic because it seems to you that the question has absolutely nothing to do with your subject, but someone asked it so maybe they know something you don't. A possible, if more devious explanation is that this is a test to see how you would handle the non sequitur in the classroom, something well-meaning and engaged students will do to you from time to time. The context is almost the same; shutting down a student's odd question will seem rude to the class as a whole, but they will also be impatient with the non sequitur, so learning how to deflect it quickly and move on is part of the law teacher's art.

You don't want to be too dismissive of something for which you see no connection, but you also don't want to seem like you're dodging the question if there really is a connection. Perhaps the question was just poorly worded; or even if it wasn't and it *is* a non sequitur, the rest of the audience won't necessarily know. The best strategy here is probably to follow up with your own question to see whether there is a connection or to find a diplomatic way to explain that there is no connection. Something like, "Hmmm, I hadn't really thought much about it because this isn't a litigation context; what particular implications were you thinking this posed?" If no help comes on the response, you might make a note and tell the questioner that you will have to think more about it and thank him or her for the thought.

The Nitpicker

Some people will either know too much about the subject of your research or just enough to be dangerous, and will ask you elaborately detailed questions about your sources, their methodology, your methodology, your sentence structure, and so on.

These questions and their answers are likely to be somewhat painful for the rest of the audience, so they are best handled with as concise an answer as possible or by bringing in the rest of the audience. If a concise answer won't work, you might say that you think it's a fascinating detail, but probably too much for the time allotted, and you and the questioner should talk about it afterward. If the answer can't be so easily deferred, you might try to bring out the bigger point to which the minute question relates, and emphasize that larger point as your response.

Sometimes, however, the questioner has something really valuable to offer, so try to keep an open mind. In Lipshaw's job talk, he had a hypothetical that depended on the failure to disclose a pending union campaign, but he had made a minor error in a description of union law that was not central to the piece. One of the listeners was a labor law expert and pointed it out. The response (with a big smile): "Thank you very much! I will make that correction and include you in the acknowledgments!"

The Hijacker

Some people have a tendency to focus on everyone else's work through the lens of their own specialty. Most of the time, these folks intend to be helpful by pointing out parallels to your work in other fields that they don't expect you to know about, parallels that may be more fully developed. Those can be great resources. Occasionally, though, a person in the audience, in the guise of the question, will drone on for several minutes about something that may or may not be related to your work in their field, suggesting along the way either that you should have known all about the work in the other field, that if you were serious you would be focused on that field instead of yours, or that it's been solved to such a degree that your work is a waste of time.

While this person is talking, you should have plenty of time to think about how your field or this particular issue is different, so that when the person finally stops talking, you can thank them and give that explanation. You can also say that you have to think more about the parallels between the two fields, and you might even ask if you can follow up with them later to hear more about their thoughts. You have to be careful with flattery, because it's often seen through, but done subtly, it can throw a questioner like this off enough to be satisfied with your answer.

The Second-Guesser

The second-guessing question seems to come up mostly, although not exclusively, with empirical work, and to a lesser extent with articles that focus on a description of history or development of a trend. Essentially, the question dismisses what you did study by asking you why you didn't study something else. Imagine that you did a study of the effects of gender on wording in contracts and someone asks you, "Why didn't you look at income level? That's what really matters."

The response to a question like this, if indeed that subject hasn't been studied by others and is an area of inquiry that fits with your work, is to put it off to future work. "I was only looking at one variable here to see if it had an impact. You're right that there are several other variables that might matter, and I will be able to focus on them in future work." You might also fall back on what your claim in this work is. If you're focused on gender and not so much on the contract interpretation, in our example, you might respond that you were not trying to definitively answer the question about all the causes that lead to the effect you focus on, but instead were trying to tease out just one aspect, perhaps one that has previously received little attention.

The Latecomer

This question comes from the faculty member who strolled in late and proceeds to pepper you with questions that you'd already answered or (worse) whose answers were provided in the missed part of your talk. Ideally your tardy would-be colleague will be filled in by his colleagues, none of whom are eager for you to have to catch him up. If not, you'll have to bring them up to speed as quickly and concisely as possible—cheerfully, and without betraying a hint of impatience.

Sorry, Wrong Number

Worse than the Non Sequitur is the "wrong number," where the faculty member's question is based on erroneous information or is otherwise ill-informed. The stress is compounded if your interrogator is unwilling to concede that she might be mistaken. You want to avoid an awkward "I think you're mistaken—No, I'm not" exchange if you can. But, in the rare case that the point is fundamental to your paper, and you're sure that you're correct, this turns into the worst of all cases: The Frontal Assault Based on Egregious Error. You have little choice but to hold to your point, lest the rest of your audience begin to wonder whether you know what you're talking about, possibly with a gentle reference back to your sources. Best case, this is standard operating procedure for that faculty member; everyone in the room has seen this movie before and views your travail simply as a rite of passage. Or perhaps the faculty member will realize she's in over her head and will defer to your superior knowledge. If not, and you can gracefully deflect the point, you might do so and move on.

How to Prepare

You ought to practice your job talk. At first, it really doesn't matter on whom you inflict it—friends, family, coworkers—you just want to get comfortable standing up and delivering your spiel within the allotted time. You might be surprised at the good questions you get from people who don't know much about your research. You'll also discover how best to provide a roadmap for your talk to help listeners follow it and how to frame the issues to make sense to someone who hasn't read your work, or at least doesn't know it as thoroughly as you do. We also think it's common to discover in practicing before a "cold" listener that the talk is far too detailed and needs to be scaled back.

As you get comfortable with simply giving the talk (and mastering any technology you'll be using), you'll want a more critical audience—one that might help you prepare for tougher questions that you might get. One resource is your law school. Law schools are often delighted that their graduates are "on the market" and would be pleased to listen to your talk and give you feedback. They might even be willing to arrange mock interviews for more practice. This would be a great opportunity not only to practice, but also to get them working for you when the AALS faculty register is distributed. Another possibility is a law school in your area; again, even if you aren't an alum, professors would likely be delighted to help an aspiring candidate get some practice.

The Exit Interview and After

The last part of your day will be a meeting with the dean. This will be a relatively short interview, and the dean will most likely assess your experience over the course of the day. She may also try to gauge your interest in the school, whether you're likely to take an offer if the school were to extend one, how likely you are to get a competing offer, and what that might mean for this school's options. Whether you are candid or coy is something only you can decide.

By the same token, this is a good opportunity to get information about the school's hiring timeline, including how many other candidates have been brought in and where you might rank within that list. Again, you'll have to decide how candid to be with these kinds of questions, but asking them may help to show that you are serious, while acknowledging that you are in demand as well.

On your way home, you might want to jot down your impressions of the day. If you printed out copies of faculty bios, you might write your impressions of those faculty members on that page, along with any notes you might want to follow up with. Get your general impressions down to help you remember the experience later on.

Unlike the interview process in practice, thank-you notes are not customary after callbacks. Chances are that you met most, if not all, of the faculty, and no one really expects candidates to keep it all straight. An e-mail or hand-written note to the dean or to the members of the faculty hiring committee is fine if you really liked the school. You might think seriously about a nice note to your faculty shepherd, recognizing the role that person will play in discussions of your candidacy and the level of preparation he or she put into your visit, and anyone else who expended particular energy in arranging or managing your visit, including law school staff with whom you had contact.

Curveballs

The callback is an intense social interaction requiring you to be "up" for almost twenty-four hours. You will largely be dealing with people who, as the mother of one of us used to say, spend most of their time with their noses in a book. Strange things may happen along the way. Even when you think you've anticipated all the strange things, something stranger will happen. Women invariably get inappropriate questions (usually from older male faculty) about marital status and family planning.

We think the best advice is to get into the moment, enjoy the experience as a social occasion, and fall back on your own best social instincts when the bizarre or untoward occurs. Even if the question from the faculty emeritus (the one who couldn't stop drooling when he spoke) violated every norm of modern discretion, not to mention federal employment laws, this is probably not the time to get on your high horse.

WHAT HAPPENS NEXT

And then, we wait. And wait, and wait, and sometimes wait some more.

Hiring new faculty is easily the most important and controversial thing that faculties do. Thus, they take this process very seriously. Not every school's process is the same, but usually, in order for the school to extend a candidate an offer, a number of things must happen. First, the committee usually discusses the candidates and votes on who should be considered by the full faculty. There may be multiple meetings, for example, to give the committee a chance to gauge the faculty sentiments in advance. Then, the full faculty is given a slate of candidates to consider, and the full faculty votes on to whom the dean is authorized to extend an offer. The faculty may authorize more than one candidate, and the dean may have discretion about whom to call, in what order, or whether to extend an offer at all. Sometimes this process will occur on a rolling basis, but sometimes it will not happen until all of the candidates have been through the callback process. However, if a candidate has an offer, the faculty may call an emergency meeting in order to act more quickly even before everyone has been through, regardless of the usual practice.

Which One of These Is Not Like the Others? Advice for Nontraditional Faculty Candidates

As our typology of candidates in chapter 2 demonstrates, there's really only one traditionally (and consistently) successful path to a law professor job, and that is being a Standard Model Super-Elite candidate. Every divergence from that set of qualifications starts to take one down a relatively nontraditional path. So what could this chapter possibly add?

Let's just say that some of us are not just more nontraditional than others, but that on any scale you might employ, as a group we're *really* nontraditional. Just as the traditional faculty candidate has had certain credentials and has followed a certain path, the traditional faculty candidate has also had a particular demographic background, namely, white, non-Hispanic, male, straight, able-bodied, and either single, or if married, the sole breadwinner, or at least the primary breadwinner. In addition to this demographic homogeneity, traditional faculty candidates have displayed some other kinds of behavioral homogeneity as well: They have approached learning and teaching in the way their professors did, and they have done research in well-established doctrinal areas, using techniques of scholarship long-accepted.[1] Finally, traditional faculty candidates have had the "Goldilocks" amount of actual law practice: not too little, and certainly not too much, but just the right amount—about two to four years.

Based on our backgrounds, we cannot provide either a definitive description of the challenges faced by those who differ from the norm in ways that we do not, nor can we offer foolproof advice for overcoming these challenges. However, we can hit some of the highlights and suggest other avenues to explore for a more complete picture.[2]

---

1. For more, and more complete, raw data on the demographics of law faculties, see the American Association of Law Schools' statistical reports at http://aals.org/resources_statistical.php. The assertions made in this section about demographics come from the most recent statistical report for the 2004–2005 year.

2. We will not cover issues about religion or about candidates with disabilities. Religion is too broad a topic because schools are more likely than other employers to have a religious mission and be legally entitled to make decisions based on the religion or the activities of candidates that conflict with religious doctrine. Disability-related issues are very complicated, and beyond our expertise.

To some extent the subjects in this chapter are legal issues in a way that the subjects in other chapters are not. Hiring choices are at least nominally governed by a number of statutes (and, for public schools, the Constitution) that protect certain groups from discrimination, and limit to some extent the bases on which hiring committees can made decisions. The American Association of Law Schools (AALS) prohibits member schools from basing hiring decisions on membership in certain groups as well. And so a person might think that none of these other characteristics will matter in the hiring process. But there are a number of tensions in this area that complicate matters.

On the one hand, law schools genuinely seek to provide legal services to the entire community, and so wish to train lawyers to do the same. Secondly, law schools also realize that there are vast untapped intellectual resources among groups that traditionally have been underrepresented in the ranks of attorneys, and work to remedy that by recruiting a more diverse student body. And thirdly, law schools generally understand their place as a pathway to social and economic power. To serve these ends, law schools work fairly hard to recruit students from all segments of the community.

It's difficult to recruit and retain those students or to train them well if the faculty looks nothing like them, or doesn't understand much about the cultures they come from. In addition to this motivation, which is really central to the mission of any law school and quite pragmatic, law schools are motivated to diversify their faculties for more idealistic reasons similar to those that prompt them to recruit students.

On the other hand, despite these motivations to reach out and to hire more diverse candidates, significant forces stand in the way of accomplishing that goal. As we've said repeatedly, faculties are like families because once a faculty member gets tenure, the rest of the faculty is stuck with that person. And so it's probably not too surprising that faculty hiring committees are very risk averse in their hiring decisions. And they tend to pick people who are much like themselves. This can easily lead to significant homogeneity. And these highly subjective decisions lend themselves to excluding those who are different. First, because it's not possible to see inside any person's head, no one outside of a person can ever know for sure what that person really intended. Second, with a group making the decision, even if one member of the group intended to exclude someone based on a protected status, that intent will not, as a legal matter, be imputed to the group unless that single person was, as a functional matter, the sole decision maker. And third, even well-meaning people can make decisions that repeatedly disadvantage members of a group without realizing that they are doing so when they base their decisions on how much they think the person will "fit" with their faculty. Finally, not all of the ways in which people differ are protected by law. For example, some states prohibit decisions made on the basis of sexual orientation, but many do not, and neither do federal statutes.

We hope that knowing about these tensions helps you navigate them more effectively, and we have some tips for specific groups as well.

WOMEN

Law, traditionally, has been a male-dominated field, and despite near parity in the numbers of law students by gender, the upper echelons of the profession remain a bastion of maleness. Law schools are no exception. The good news for women is that this is changing fast, and there is not nearly as much of a glass ceiling in academia as there once was. The bad news is that, in many ways, there's still a long way to go, especially when it comes to issues of family and what has been termed "the maternal wall." And to the extent that schools have tried recently to hire more women, some may be suffering from "diversity fatigue": We've hired enough of "them"; now we can go back to focusing on male candidates.

The ideal law professor, the picture the hiring committee usually has in its mind, is a person who can focus nearly exclusively on research and writing, churning out paper after paper, all of which place in top journals. At the same time, the ideal professor is able to teach two classes a semester so well that students will be able to practice in that area immediately upon finishing the class, can help students in various extracurricular activities outside of class, and can help the students get jobs upon graduation. The ideal professor also has nearly unlimited time to devote to committee work within the law faculty, and also for the university the law school is a part of. Finally, the ideal law professor is the dictator for his household, never needing to consult with anyone else about issues related to career, like what job to take, how much time to work, or where to live.

Despite the fact that there isn't a man in America who fits this stereotype (even guys have to sleep sometime, and very few are household dictators), the stereotypical man devotes his energies to work first, and other areas only second. The stereotypical woman, on the other hand, is presumed to devote her energies to work secondarily. At some point, the stereotype goes, the woman will marry (in our stereotype she will marry a man), she will subordinate her career to his, and she will have children. That family will be the primary focus of her energies, and she will stop working, although even if she did not, there is so little energy left for work that it comes in a distant second in terms of priorities. Moreover, she will not be able to make decisions for the household. And so, in terms of long-term investment and employer flexibility, the stereotypical male seems the better bet—a higher rate of return for a much longer period and a greater amount of control over the faculty member's life by the employer.

While these stereotypes may seem ridiculous, and very few people still consciously believe in them wholeheartedly, these stereotypes often sit in the backs of people's heads as benchmarks, subtly influencing their perceptions of the candidates they interview. And it's not just men who hold these stereotypes; women hold many of the same or similar kinds of judgments. Female candidates who have expectations or experiences that differ from those of women already on the faculty may be judged quite harshly by the women who have gone before, particularly if those who went before feel that they made sacrifices to reach their current positions.

There are also some views about how women differ from men in the ways that they process information and relate to people. Some studies suggest that women tend to be more contextual and relational in the way they process information and communicate.[3] Legal education, in contrast, is traditionally very hierarchical, the process centered on the Socratic method, with the professor pushing individual students to puzzle out a general rule from what they've read to prepare for class. That technique does not work well for everyone, but it's often perceived by tenured faculty as the only legitimate way to present information. To the extent that you might approach the material in a different way, or that you might be perceived to approach the material differently, some faculty members might discount your abilities. Keep in mind that the traditional way for schools to hire new faculty was to hire those who were at the tops of their classes, and people at the tops of their classes were those who thrived with the Socratic method.

Likewise, your potential areas of teaching or writing can present some challenges. There are some areas that are taught more often by women than men:[4] Women and the Law or Feminist Jurisprudence, Critical Legal Studies or Critical Race Theory, Legal Drafting and Legal Research and Writing, and Family and Juvenile Law. There are some areas where very few women teach: Admiralty, Law and Economics, Corporate Finance, and Antitrust, for example.[5] Of the most common first-year courses, women make up 32 percent of Civil Procedure professors, 26 percent of Contracts professors, 23 percent of Constitutional Law professors, 30 percent of Criminal Law professors, 33 percent of Property professors, 30 percent of Tort Law professors, and 57 percent of Legal Writing professors. Some of this is because women make up only 37 percent of all faculties. Still, they are underrepresented in most of the core courses. And this presents something of a double bind. If you want to teach a female-dominated course, schools may understand that desire, but may discount the importance of the course. If you don't want to teach a female-dominated course, on the other hand, schools will value the course more, but may distrust your ability or true interest in the area.

Finally, there are some special concerns for scholarship. The areas in which people write are often similar to the areas in which they teach, and so

---

3. The classic work is Carol Gilligan, *In a Different Voice* (1982).

4. The statistics on the gender makeup of teachers in these areas can be found in the AALS' statistical reports. The most recent is at http://www.aals.org/statistics/0506/0506_T10_subj_frq.html.

5. The other subjects where women make up 20 percent or fewer of the professors are Aviation and Space Law, Creditors' and Debtors' Rights, Entertainment Law, Equity, Government Contracts, Insurance Law, Jurisprudence, Law and Accounting, Legal History, National Security Law, Oil and Gas, Regulated Industries, Sports Law, and Trade Regulation. Women constitute over 90 percent of those teaching Feminist Legal Theory and Women and the Law. Women comprise over 60 percent of those teaching Critical Legal Studies, Critical Race Theory, Disability Law, Family Law, Juvenile Law, and Poverty Law.

there are some areas that women write in disproportionate to their numbers, and some areas in which women's voices are rarely heard. There is an added dimension here, as well. Our notion of quality scholarship is in some flux, which brings good news and bad news. Once, descriptive and doctrinal scholarship was considered the pinnacle of serious work. The feminist and critical legal studies movement have opened the field for new techniques and broader focuses for scholarship, to some extent; and Law and Economics, empirical work, and other interdisciplinary approaches have benefited. And so there are more subjects and more techniques of study that are considered legitimate than there once were. Still, however, some alternatives are more established than others.

And so, what can you do with this somewhat depressing information? Just be aware that those stereotypes and pitfalls may be out there. It may mean that you need to work a little harder to demonstrate that you are committed to the rigors of scholarship and that you have thought about where you are going from here. The growing numbers of women entering academia, and the diversity among them, however, show that things continue to improve.

Also, take some gender-related warnings (perhaps even ours) with a grain of salt. Just to give one example, related to the work/life balance issue, McCormick has three children, and at various times was told that she really should put off having kids until after tenure; that if she had kids, she should wait to go on the market until they were older so that people would not assume she was trying to go part time; that it's not possible to balance work and family in academia; that she shouldn't seek any kind of maternity leave before tenure; and that she wasn't entitled to any kind of maternity leave. And, of course, none of these things has actually been true, or at least not entirely true. In fact, when she demonstrated that she could be pregnant, have kids, and still publish with regularity, people stopped offering these kinds of advice.

Now that does not mean you shouldn't pay attention to these kinds of statements. To some extent they can serve as a barometer to the type of faculty you are dealing with. You may not want to be a part of a group that would assume any of these things, or that might not support their colleagues who occasionally encounter difficulties in life. Most faculties will routinely do so, covering classes when colleagues or members of their families have medical problems, and even allowing light loads or leaves, extending the tenure clock for pretenure folks who need that because of some serious issue. And commonly, schools are doing the same kinds of things for faculty members when they first have or adopt a baby. Mostly, these benefits are offered to women, but under the Family Medical Leave Act, they should be available to men, too. And the more men take advantage of them, the less this will be viewed as a woman's issue.

PEOPLE OF COLOR

The news for people of color is in some ways more sobering and in others more hopeful. Law schools have a pretty poor record both of hiring candidates of

color and of retaining and promoting them. While the gender gap in promotion has dwindled, the racial gap has remained.[6] And there have been some
large and well-publicized tenure battles faced by African American professors, in particular. The more hopeful note for candidates of color is that the
AALS and its member schools are working harder to recruit, retain, and promote professors of color. As of this writing, diversity is still a hot topic, and we
understand the perception among candidates of color that they may well have
an advantage, at least in getting interviews.[7] There is a very long way to go,
however, and diversity fatigue is a common obstacle to progress here, as well.

Stereotypes operate for candidates of color, and they differ depending on
the group the candidate is a member of. The common denominator is that
candidates of color may not be viewed as competent teachers or scholars, and
some schools may even hire without any expectation that the candidate will
succeed. They may be expected to teach and write in areas of special interest,
like critical race studies, and then their work becomes minimized as a result.
Work in other areas may also be discounted.

Candidates of color may be less likely than their white counterparts to
have been encouraged to consider careers in academia, and so may not have
developed the networks or strategies for scholarship that will help them succeed. Some schools have developed fellowships or LL.M. programs geared
specifically toward minority candidates to provide these kinds of resources;
examples include Harvard's Lewis and Hamilton Fellowships, the University of Wisconsin's Hastie Fellowship, Georgetown's Graduate Fellowship for
Future Law Professors, and the University of Iowa's Faculty Fellows Program.
Professor Gabriel J. (Jack) Chin and Professor Denise Morgan edited a comprehensive guide to breaking into law teaching that appeared most recently in
the *Michigan Journal of Race & Law*.[8] There are also a number of blogs and
Listservs devoted to issues of law professors of color that may provide good
information and support.[9]

None of us is a professor of color. We never experienced what it is like to
look different from the predominant race of our particular society. Neverthe-

---

6. AALS Comm. on Recruitment and Retention of Minority Law Teachers, The
Racial Gap in Promotion to Tenure of Law Professors: Report of the Committee
on Recruitment and Retention of Minority Law Teachers—Committee Commentary (2005), http://www.aals.org/documents/racialgap.pdf; *see also* Richard A. Write,
The Promotion, Retention, and Tenuring of Law School Faculty: Comparing
Faculty Hired in 1990 and 1991 to Faculty Hired in 1996 and 1997 (2004), http://www
.aals.org/documents/2005recruitmentreport.pdf.

7. Our source for this is a 2007–2008 visiting assistant professor (VAP) at a highly ranked
school, who advised us that the three black candidates who had been VAPs at that school
received in the neighborhood of forty-five invitations each for the 2007 FRC. As noted earlier, this is an astronomical number of invitations.

8. *Breaking into the Academy: The 2002–2004 Michigan Journal of Race & Law Guide
for Aspiring Law Professors*, 7 Mich. J. Race & L. 457 (2002). Denise Morgan has since
tragically passed away at far too young an age.

9. *E.g.*, AALS Section on Minority Groups, http://www.aals.org/services.php (click on
Sections, then on Minority Groups).

less, we've talked to some of our colleagues who are, and we gingerly offer the following:

> You will have special issues related to the area on which you choose to write and teach, and even how you write and teach, all tinged with some controversy and debate, because you are a candidate of color, and the issues are just as likely to come from minority or majority constituencies. We feel quite certain that traditional white male candidates almost never have to deal with this issue at all. One view, for example, says that there's an advantage in a minority candidate's expression of a desire to fill teaching and scholarship niches other than in matters of race policy. Another view seems to find it a cop-out to make the instrumental choice to focus on racially neutral topics as a way of avoiding controversy. Moreover, there is substantive debate over the appropriate form of race scholarship—particularly what is referred to as "voice scholarship."[10] We will decline to take a position on this, other than to make the fairly obvious observation that this is, for better or worse, a special issue for candidates of color.

> We won't try to do a sociological analysis of the issues of minority hiring (or affirmative action) in a time when most sensible people ought to know that expressions with a public meaning suggesting racism have a quick and negative consequence for the speaker. Nor can we say that the phenomenon we are about to describe is a subtle form of racism, a misplaced "liberal" paternalism, or colorblind application of the same faculty preconceptions that apply to nonminority candidates. But the perception goes as follows: Even more than with traditional white candidates, everyone wants a super-elite professor of color. Hence, a candidate who has been "whitewashed" by a degree from Harvard, Yale, or Stanford has a leg up, even more relatively to racial peers than to white candidates. For example, one perception is that candidates of color who would otherwise be Standard Model Elite (see chapter 2—having graduated from one of the elite schools but not a Super Elite) do not need to have a publication record. Indeed, the observation in the 2007-08 season was that Standard Model Elite (Of Color) candidates, even without publications, got good placements.

> Racial affinity isn't everything. We've reached the point (we hope) where merely being identified as a member of a particular minority doesn't mean that one is also presumptively tagged with a particular set of beliefs. And when people of mixed backgrounds like Barack Obama are among the most admired in the world, we might have gotten beyond all the superficial differences. But the reality is that racial politics still exist, albeit at perhaps a more sophisticated level, and now with far more equal opportunity to engage in them. We want to tread lightly here, but think it's sensible to point out that not everyone who shares your racial or

---

10. For a good summary of these issues, see Monica Bell, *The Obligation Thesis: Understanding the Persistent "Black Voice" in Modern Legal Scholarship*, 68 U. PITT. L. REV. 643 (2007).

ethnic heritage is necessarily your friend. There's no reason to suspect that professors of color are any more or less subject to the normal human flaws than their white counterparts. Accordingly, many will be wonderful confidantes, mentors, counselors, supporters, or advocates. But some will not.

> At the end of the day, you still have to write, if not to get hired, then to succeed.

SEXUAL ORIENTATION/IDENTITY

Issues of sexual orientation and identity present unique challenges. Some states still allow hiring decisions to be made based on a person's sexual orientation or identity, and federal law has generally been interpreted to allow this as well. On the other hand, the AALS prohibits its member schools from making hiring decisions on the basis of sexual orientation,[11] unless they are schools with a religious focus where the religion forbids same-sex sexual activity. And so some schools are very open and supportive places for gay, lesbian, bisexual, and transgendered (GLBT) people to work, while others openly exclude these people. Some schools also occupy a middle ground, lacking faculty who are gay, lesbian, bisexual, or transgendered (or at least faculty who are out), but not explicitly excluding faculty on that ground.

It's fairly easy to tell which schools are at the extremes, but it's more difficult to tell how welcoming the schools in the middle might be. One way to gauge that is to check whether there is a GLBT student organization. A school without such an organization is less likely to be a supportive place to work. Another way to ensure that any school interested in you is going to welcome you is to include in your resume membership in any GLBT organizations or scholarship on sexual orientation or gender identity issues if you have done any.

The AALS has a section on sexual orientation and gender identity issues,[12] and its Web page contains more useful information and links.

OLDER PEOPLE (READ "LONGTIME PRACTITIONERS")

This isn't really about older people, because we can't think of any reason why a person who waits until late in life to go to law school, attends Harvard, Yale, or Stanford, edits the law review, graduates in the top five percent, and clerks for a Supreme Court Justice, then works for a Wall Street firm for two years

---

11. Although the bylaws do not list sexual identity separately, that might be included within the definition of "sex" and so covered that way.

12. See its January 2009 newsletter at http://www.aals.org/documents/sections/sexual/SOGIINewsletter(Jan2009ConferenceIssue).pdf.

while publishing a piece in the *Michigan Law Review*, wouldn't be a Standard Model Super-Elite candidate. We just don't know many people like that.

What is far more likely is that you are a long-time practitioner who has visions of a leafy campus, a bike ride to work, ditching your business attire, and having a bevy of grateful students at your knee, absorbing it all as you pontificate wisely based on your years of accumulated wisdom. One of us (Lipshaw) has indeed plied this road, and has written about it elsewhere.[13] Perhaps the best thing here is simply to note some of the highlights (or lowlights):

> Most academic lawyers presume that the cranial synapses necessary to theorize like a professor suffer atrophy after about five or six years of practice. Combined with the substantial likelihood that you've been raking in the big bucks while they've been toiling for peanuts (which means they are looking for reasons why you couldn't possibly jump in and do what they've spent a career doing), don't expect to be taken seriously with anything less than some first-rate theoretical writing published in a recognized journal. In fact, even a *single* article may well be regarded as something of a fluke. Whatever we've said about it being a writing job goes double or triple here.

> Assuming you get interviews at the AALS Faculty Recruitment Conference (FRC), you will be a curiosity. Do everything you can to minimize the telling of your life story, and keep the focus on your scholarship.

> Understand the dichotomous nature of your practical experience. Lots of people will tell you what a shame it is that there isn't more practical experience within the academy. Some of those people may actually believe it. By and large, until you've established scholarly chops, the practice experience weighs against you. But if you can get over the hurdle, and become perceived as a scholar, the practice experience immediately becomes a significant positive.

> Get used to the strange etiquette of the academy. Promptness, follow-up, and decisiveness are all hallmarks of successful practitioners, whether in law firms or in-house. They are not hallmarks of normal academic behavior.

> Work the networks. Obviously it's a positive if you can land a visiting professorship. Get active on the blogs (intelligent comments may lead to an invitation to guest blog). Go to the AALS annual meeting in January and attend the paper sessions. Go to conferences like the Law and Society meeting. Work the room. Schmooze.

Lipshaw practiced longer than the model expects, practicing for twenty-six years before going to his first AALS FRC. It can be done, but it's a long shot. Perseverance is required, although it is not always sufficient to guarantee success.

---

13. Jeffrey M. Lipshaw, *Memo to Lawyers: How Not to "Retire and Teach,"* 30 N.C. CENT. L. REV. 151 (2008).

TEACHING OR WRITING IN NONTRADITIONAL AREAS OR AGAINST STEREOTYPE

Aside from status, other kinds of diversity figure into the equation as well. Diversity of thought, research, and academic freedom are cornerstones of higher education in the United States. In fact, our system of tenure is designed to promote these things. But, of course, there are few constraints on a school at the point it is making the decision to hire a person. And so the less traditional (or stereotypical) a candidate's outlook, teaching, or scholarship, or the more a candidate is viewed as a potentially divisive element, the less likely a school will consider the candidate. This conservatism is particularly strong for law schools because most law schools shy away from hiring candidates they think may have trouble achieving tenure.

To the extent that your interests diverge from what might be expected of you (whether rationally expected or not), be careful to clearly articulate how those interests fit into the core mission of the law school, and how they will supplement what the school already provides. This sort of reflection demonstrates that you have a desire to contribute constructively, not divisively, and this desire by itself can mitigate concerns the hiring committee might have.

A MATCHED SET

Getting back to a stereotype discussed in the section on women, the ideal faculty candidate is the sole decision maker for career and life issues. However, in real life, many of us have intimate partners with whom we share decisions, and occasionally, a couple may be on the job market at the same time. This is a particularly difficult situation to be in. Given the fact that the hiring market is so tight, it can be very difficult for two candidates to get jobs at the same school or even in the same general geographic area.

This difficulty is compounded by the fact that some faculties hesitate to hire couples. Schools want to maximize their options, and hiring two candidates as a package will often limit the school's flexibility, not just in hiring, but in future treatment as well. Some faculties hesitate beyond that, also. Some members of the faculty may not believe that both members of the couple are equally well qualified, will be equally productive scholars, or equally good fits with the rest of the faculty. And the school won't want to get "stuck" with the poorer candidate. Even beyond that, because faculties govern themselves, they may hesitate to bring in people with an established alliance. That alliance could disrupt faculty politics much more than the addition of a single person or two people who wouldn't necessarily be allies, to say nothing of what a bitter divorce can do to a faculty.

As a result, if both of you do find yourselves on the market at the same time, you might consider whether to tell schools that you interview with. You might consider not bringing it up at all until after you have received an offer.

That is the point at which you have the greatest bargaining power, and the school will not have discounted you without giving you a chance. If you want to weed out those schools that wouldn't even consider both of you, though, you might bring it up at your meat market interview. In essence, this is probably the trickiest situation to be in, but people have done it, and so you shouldn't let this stop you from pursuing a teaching job. Finally, because some law schools *seek out* teaching couples, you might make a special effort to find out which schools do, and contact them directly.

POLITICAL CONSERVATIVES (AND POLITICAL LIBERALS)

There is a view, not entirely unwarranted, that law school faculties are, on the whole, politically liberal. There is a corresponding view that because of the perceived leftward tilt of legal academy, self-identifying legal conservatives will have their politics held against them by hiring committees and law school faculties. At the very least, it is thought that while faculties might grudgingly tolerate economic conservatives or libertarians in corporate or commercial law areas, being a self-identified social conservative, devoutly religious, or a conservative in areas like criminal or constitutional law sounds the death knell for anyone's candidacy.

We think that the perception both of the political tilt of faculties as well as the effect it might have on candidates who don't conform to a particular political orthodoxy can be overstated. The authors' views span the political spectrum, as do the views of their respective faculties. None of us has ever seen a candidate's liberalism or conservatism held against her, though we have heard anecdotal accounts of it happening. Faculties care most about hiring thoughtful, collegial people who will enhance the intellectual atmosphere of the school and excite and inspire students to learn. Partisan politics is not normally something that is taken into account, in the authors' experience. Note the "collegial" part, however. Whether you're liberal or conservative, if you get into a heated political argument during a job interview, it will likely be held against you.

That said, and because we are sure there are exceptions, if you have been a lifelong Federalist Society member and a Republican Party activist, you might have to satisfy your would-be colleagues that you are not doctrinaire or a thoughtless ideologue, especially if you are interviewing in the Northeast or in parts of the West Coast. At other law schools in other parts of the country, not only would your activities not raise eyebrows, they might be considered strengths. (At those schools, candidates who have worked for NARAL or the ACLU might have to satisfy some faculty that they aren't wild-eyed revolutionaries.) One benefit of the on-campus interview is that you can develop personal relationships with people that will make it difficult to pigeonhole you according to what your politics may be (or seem).

If you get questions about your writings or your politics, try to handle them with the grace you would any other difficult or even inappropriate comment or question. When Denning was on the market, he was a candidate at an urban law school in the Northeast. After his callback, the hiring chair contacted him and said that a couple of faculty members raised questions about some of Denning's writings on the Second Amendment. Denning was asked to provide a statement summarizing his views on the extent to which the Amendment guaranteed an individual's right to keep and bear arms.[14] As he talked to the hiring chair, it dawned on Denning that the faculty members were trying to make sure that he wasn't sympathetic with antigovernment militia groups much in the news at the time. (Denning always suspected that being a southerner was an additional strike!) Denning dutifully wrote a short summary of his views, disclaimed sympathy for Tim McVeigh, and the issue went away.

Of course, if you are passionate about your politics, and find yourself out of step with the views of the faculty, the students, and even the surrounding community, then you might ask yourself whether that school is right for you. On our own faculties, though, we have a range of political views. The better faculties will acknowledge and celebrate that intellectual diversity, even while disagreeing.

---

14. The hiring chair was apologetic. "Of course," Denning remembers the chair remarking, "you've said all of this in your articles, which they ought to have read."

Offer and Acceptance: Handling Job Offers

With time, talent, and a little bit of luck, one of your callbacks will become a full-fledged job offer. It generally sounds something like this:

> [Telephone rings.]
> **CANDIDATE:** Hello.
> **DEAN:** Hello, Candidate. This is Dean Loblaw. How are you?
> **CANDIDATE:** I'm fine. How are you?
> **DEAN:** I'm fine, too. I'm calling to tell you that our faculty has voted to invite you to join our faculty.
> **CANDIDATE:** Oh, thank God. I accept.
> **DEAN:** Do you have any questions for me?
> **CANDIDATE:** No. When do I start?

Of course, what Candidate has failed to do here is learn that she has just committed to working for minimum wage and covering a section of corporate tax. What Candidate is likely to find out later is that this was the time to ask for things that she might not get later. Yes, you're grateful, even worshipful; but you need to temper the gratitude with a healthy dose of self-interest.

This chapter attempts to help you do just that. In it, we attempt to explain the structure of the job offer; specifically, what it will include, what is presumptively negotiable, and what may or may not be negotiable. We also discuss what we euphemistically refer to as "delicate matters," like the unfortunately named "trailing spouse" and exploding offers. As with much else in this book, we can offer only the broadest and most general overview. The devil is, as always, in the details; and those details may vary widely from school to school. That said, the thrust of this chapter can be summed up: (1) Ask for what you want at the point of offer, instead of later; (2) Even if the answer is "no," it doesn't hurt to ask, as long as you don't ask for too much; and (3) Get whatever deal you negotiate in writing.

WHAT THE JOB OFFER WILL USUALLY INCLUDE

The Pay

As a general proposition, most starting salaries for an assistant or an associate professor at a law school are much higher than for, say, an assistant professor of English. (This is why our university colleagues often think that law professors are overpaid and underworked.) But, relative to what one could make in practice, they flatten out quickly. Just like in practice, some well-known professors at elite schools make large sums of money, but this is the exception rather than the norm. But surely you haven't embarked on this journey to get rich! That said, many of us find it difficult to put a price on the flexibility and autonomy that come with the job.

One of the services the Society of American Law Teachers (SALT) provides to the community at large is an annual salary survey.[1] The SALT survey doesn't give starting salary information, but it does provide information from many schools, and breaks it out by assistant, associate, and full professor ranks. We can't vouch for the accuracy of the information, but it does seem to reflect that (1) elite schools tend to pay more than others (the reported figures for assistant professors at Harvard and Michigan, for example, are $150,000 and $166,000, respectively), and (2) salaries vary regionally as one might expect, given relative costs of living.[2]

The Perks

The main perk of being a law professor is the flexibility and autonomy that you will have, coupled with the rewarding experience of teaching your students. Given the pay relative to practice, if you don't find those things satisfying or attractive, then you might want to ask yourself again whether this is the job for you.

Nevertheless, law schools want to hire the very best people possible, meaning those folks who are bright, motivated, competent teachers, and who will be productive long after tenure. As anyone who has ever sat on an appointments committee can attest, schools must compete for such candidates. Despite the fact that each year many more candidates go on the market than there are academic positions, there are a relatively small number of truly exceptional prospects—even discounting the outliers for whom the elite schools compete. Therefore, law schools offer nonsalary perks that you will want to ask about when negotiating the offer. We discuss a few of the common ones in this section; in the next sections we single out a few as "presumptively negotiable" as well as some that are "possibly negotiable." Despite this lengthy

---

1. http://www.saltlaw.org/contents/view/salarysurvey.
2. Faculty Lounge, *Law School and University Faculty Salary Data: A Compensation Compendium* (updated June 25, 2009), http://www.thefacultylounge.org/2009/04/university-faculty-salary-information-redux-serious-data-for-the-seriously-curious.html.

list, don't be fooled into thinking that your decision should be based on each one. Go with your gut and the big picture. Use this list simply as a resource to negotiate once you are comfortable that you could accept an offer from this school more generally.

> *Summer research dollars.* It is now commonplace for schools to offer summer stipends as incentives for doing research and writing over the summer. These vary in their structure. Some schools provide for an extra month's pay. Others pay a flat rate, generally somewhere between $8,000 and $15,000. Sometimes this is paid out in installments, with a holdback to ensure completion and submission of an article (the holdback is paid out once the article is placed). Some schools pay a stipend, plus a "prestige bonus" for placing the article in a top-twenty or top-ten law journal. Some schools award stipends on a competitive basis; at others, they're more like entitlements. Most schools have some sort of accountability mechanism: You have to present your paper to the faculty; you have to have published in the previous year to be eligible going forward, and so on. Some schools provide stipends to new hires for class preparation with no requirement that you produce a paper that year. Some schools have a "residency" requirement for the stipend, requiring you to be at school or at least in town for the duration.

> *Health care.* Universities generally offer health care to employees and their families. These plans vary widely. It makes a difference whether your institution is public or private; it may also matter if your institution is a faith-based institution, which may not cover things like contraceptives under their plan. Most universities have a fact sheet that outlines the highlights of the plan. Don't ignore these, even if you are one of the "young invincibles" who laugh at danger by forgoing health insurance. Universities sometimes offer life and disability insurance up to a certain amount, and then offer the opportunity to purchase additional coverage at favorable rates. You'll want to compare these rates to others that you might purchase elsewhere, but once you take the job, consider purchasing extra disability insurance, especially if you have a family. And pay attention to the university's disability policy as well, especially if you will be your family's primary earner.

> *403(b)(7).* This is the equivalent of the 401(k)—a plan that permits you to shelter pretax money in an investment account for retirement. Few universities offer defined benefit pensions any longer; even if yours is one of the few survivors, you should also put money in the 403(b) each month.

> *Reciprocal tuition waivers.* If you have children, or might want to one day, the prospect of sending one or more of them to college can give even the thriftiest parent nightmares when the likely future cost of higher education is calculated. Many universities, however, participate in consortia of similar schools that waive tuition for children of faculty from schools in their consortium. This is potentially a huge benefit, especially if the consortium contains desirable, competitive, and expensive schools.

> *Administrative assistance.* You will usually share an assistant with a number of other professors, perhaps as many as four or five. If you are coming from practice where you had a dedicated assistant, or one who worked for you and associates you supervised, then having to share might be more of a burden than if you've *never* had an assistant. In truth, the importance of assistants is probably not what it once was. Most of the law professors we know do their own word processing, using their assistants only when editing documents; and with electronic submissions, one needn't delegate the task of running off multiple copies of lengthy articles any longer. That said, a good assistant is invaluable, as Denning discovered when he served as appointments committee chair; moreover, your assistant can still help with tasks such as mailing out article reprints and navigating the arcane world of obtaining travel reimbursement from university budget offices.

> *Research and travel budgets.* We think that it's a good sign if you've been offered a job by a school that finds it necessary to budget money for travel and research for its faculty. Budgeting suggests that there are enough faculty members engaged in those activities that some rationing is required. (Of course, it could simply mean that money is tight. That's worth investigating as you do your due diligence on the school.) In some cases, the budget is what you can spend without prior authorization, with the understanding that the dean will approve reasonable requests. In other cases, schools might have a policy to pay for travel to any conference at which you are presenting or speaking (assuming the hosting institution is not picking up the tab), so that you can save your budget for conferences that you simply want to attend.

> *Book budget.* Some law schools give professors a dedicated allowance for the purchase of books. Sometimes these will go to the library; other times, the professor is allowed to keep the book or books on permanent loan. If the latter, the books are technically the law school's property and have to be returned if you leave the school. At other schools, the books are the professor's property and aren't catalogued in the school's library.

> *Research assistant hours.* Another common way law schools support faculty scholarship is by permitting you to hire one or more students as research assistants for a certain number of hours a week (usually twenty to twenty-five). The students earn money and have the opportunity to develop a close working relationship with a faculty member. You, in theory, get research aid. (Whether this will be helpful for you and your research is another matter. Our experience is that research assistants perform best when given discrete, supervised tasks. Of course, that requires you to, well, supervise them.)

> *Offprint reimbursement.* Most schools will also reimburse you for the cost of reprints that you order and will bear the cost of mailing them to colleagues at other schools. If you are prolific, and if you disseminate your scholarship far and wide, as you should, this is no small perk.

PRESUMPTIVELY NEGOTIABLE ITEMS

As noted above, salary flexibility can range from nearly nonexistent (at state schools) to downright pliable. Even at schools with lockstep pay scales, most deans will have *something* to use to make their school attractive to candidates it hopes to hire. We mention the most common ones below.

Course Package

An understanding about what courses you will be teaching can save you headaches in the coming years. Deans and associate deans are particularly keen to ensure that required courses and bar courses are offered at regular intervals so that students will be able to take them before graduating. They are sometimes *less* concerned that myriad specialized seminars are offered that enable you to indulge your research interests. Don't be shy about asking for "Law and Literature," "Constitutional Theory," or "In-House Counsel Practice" courses at the outset. And if you really don't feel comfortable teaching Remedies, Property, Professional Responsibility, or another course that senior faculty are always trying to give up, you need to let that be known as well. Sure, you may have been hired as the new Constitutional Law professor, but don't tune out just as the dean gets to the part about how you're also going to teach a section of Legal Writing or Wills, Trusts, and Estates. (Not that there's anything wrong with those courses!)

Occasionally, you'll be asked, at the outset, to take one for the team, and teach a new prep for a year or so, with vague promises that someone will replace you before long. In this category are the equally vague promises that, well, we can't let you teach International Human Rights *this* year, but Professor So-and-So will probably retire soon, and you'll have dibs on that course. In both cases, you ought to get it in writing. At the very least, having the piece of writing may give the dean's conscience a twinge when she later reneges on the promise.[3]

Most law schools will not be able give you four upper-level elective courses that perfectly mesh with your research interests. That is why it is important to think hard before your interviews about courses that you either wouldn't mind teaching, though you may not write in those areas, or in which you have little or no background, but might enjoy becoming expert in.

This is probably also as good a place as any to mention that you ought to cultivate a close and friendly relationship with the associate dean for academic affairs. This person will be responsible for drawing up the class schedules from year to year, and has discretion in the assignment of classrooms, as

---

3. Even if the dean is no longer there, having the piece of paper at least provides corroborating evidence for the *new* dean that some kind of deal was in place, and that you're not just making it up.

well as the days and times classes are taught. You want this person to have a good opinion of you. The best way for that to occur is not to be the problem faculty member. You might consider taking the hit early and volunteering for the early morning, late afternoon, or evening class. You will signal that you're a team player, not a prima donna, and are willing to place individual comfort second to institutional needs. The associate dean will appreciate this and will repay your sacrifice in the future, perhaps giving you a writing day off at the beginning or end of a week or accommodating your preference for particular times or specific classrooms. You may even find the associate dean able to help you secure that seminar that you want to teach.

Stipend for the First Summer

In the next chapter, we'll exhort you to move as soon as you can after you've accepted the job, but certainly no later than early summer. You're going to be busier than you can imagine, and you'll need a lot more time than you might expect to prepare for your first semester. But wait, you might be asking, what will I do for money? At some schools, your contract will not begin until classes do. Thus you might be there, at the school, working, but not drawing a paycheck. This does not mean that you'll be forced to fall back on undergraduate/law school survival skills, like how to live on nothing but ramen and coffee.

Law school deans anticipate this problem, and, though they may not advertise it, they often have authority to grant a summer research stipend even for a new hire not yet technically on the payroll. Some schools also define the stipend broadly, encompassing class preparation as well as scholarship. Of course, if you hire the money, as Coolidge once said, you've got to have something to show for it. But you ought to be writing the summer before your first class anyway, and accepting the obligation by accepting the stipend may be just the incentive you need to ensure that happens even if the terms of your stipend don't require a finished article.

Summer Conference Expenses

Every summer, the Association of American Law Schools (AALS) holds a three-day program for entry-level law professors. Many schools will insist that you go, but if its not in your offer letter, be sure to put it in. There may also be other conferences you wish to attend; a number of general subject conferences and conferences for other disciplines are held in the summer. You will have enough to do that you don't want to go to too many, but a conference can be a great way to jump start your scholarship and to build up your networks.

Light Load for First Year

A light first-year load was once a benefit offered only at elite schools. With almost every accredited law school interested in having faculty produce *some* scholarship, though, a light load for the first year has become much more commonplace. Support for scholarship ought to be on your must-ask list at the meat market. Usually schools will mention light loads then. Still, some schools may not advertise them. Don't assume that you're going to be light-loaded during the first year. Ask for it. You might also ask whether you can choose which semester to take the light load; some people prefer it in the spring. Again, you help your case if you can demonstrate that you have a writing project in progress that you will use that extra time to polish up. It bears repeating though: Don't fritter away your summer, thinking that you'll have loads of extra time to write during your light load. As we note in the next chapter, you'll likely feel that you're barely treading water preparing for one class, and will spend no small amount of time worrying how in the world you would juggle *two* classes the following semester.

Moving Expenses

This may not sound like much of a perk, but if you're moving an entire household across the country, the cost of a move can be significant (often in the $10,000–$20,000 range, sometimes more). Some state schools will try to cut costs here, imposing an unreasonably low rate of reimbursement, or forcing you to forgo an "exclusive" move—meaning that only your stuff is on the truck. Moving itself is stressful enough without worrying that your low bidder is going to damage, lose, fold, spindle, or mutilate your stuff. Try to get them to reimburse reasonable expenses of the move, instead of imposing some arbitrary cap. Schools may require you to get a couple of bids, but will reimburse your expenses, while requiring you to repay a share of those expenses if you leave their school before a certain time. You might even offer to do that if it means you can escape some low cap.

POSSIBLY NEGOTIABLE ITEMS

Salary

This is a touchy subject with many schools. State schools may have fairly rigid pay scales that force candidates to begin at a certain rate and progress in lockstep with those of similar experience. Some deans will simply be unwilling to negotiate, fearful of compressing the salaries of more senior faculty members. Still, it never hurts to ask as long as you do it very delicately. You might ask the dean or a faculty member at the school whether salary is negotiable. If that person briskly says no, then there is no harm done, but if the answer is yes, then you have started the conversation. You should compare the salary offered to the expected cost of living in an area. The SALT survey of faculty salaries, mentioned earlier, may be helpful here.[4] Not every school participates in that survey, but you should get a general idea of the ranges in your region.

---

4. *Supra* note 1.

Research/Travel Budget

If you want more, you should be able to demonstrate why you need it. Do some research on conferences in your field; find out which might it be helpful to attend, even if the purpose is purely networking. What projects have you initiated or planned that require additional resources? Not only will this exercise help you allocate your time during the coming year, it will send the right signals to your potential employer—even if no additional money is forthcoming.

Starting Rank

If you have had some significant experience prior to starting your academic career, you might be able to argue for starting at a higher rank, at, say, the associate professor level, rather than as an assistant professor. Doing so could achieve any one of several things. First, it might cut the time to tenure, if you're in a hurry and think that you can meet the publication requirements. Second, the higher rank might mean a higher salary, depending on whether raises accompany promotion.

What counts as "significant experience"? It might include judicial clerkships, time as a visiting assistant professor or fellow, government service, or even significant private practice experience.

Note, however, that you might not want to push for the higher starting rank for political reasons. Some faculty members (and university officials, who think tenure standards at law schools are already lax) might make trouble later by holding you to higher standards than they would a candidate who began at the usual rank. You might not even know who these folks are at the time, which complicates things. Sadly, jumping the rank queue may be particularly hazardous for female and minority candidates.

Time to Tenure

As discussed in chapter 1, the law school tenure track at most law schools anticipates an entry-level candidate going up for a vote in years five or six, with tenure effective at the start of the following year. If you are publishing ahead of schedule and your teaching is coming along, you may be encouraged to go up in year four (though anecdotal evidence suggests that university provosts are, for financial reasons, beginning to push back on early tenure grants in law schools). If you successfully negotiate an increase in rank, you may also negotiate a shortened time to tenure, at least at institutions where tenure is awarded independently of a promotion from assistant to associate professor. While you *might* be able to shave a year off the tenure track as an entry-level, the warnings about increased expectations accompanying coming in as an associate professor apply here, too. Credit for years taught is much more important for lateral hires, a subject that deserves separate treatment.[5]

---

5. *See generally* Paul M. Secunda, *Tales of a Law Professor Lateral Nothing*, 30 U. MEM. L. REV. 125 (2008).

Credit for Prior Writing

In addition to presumptive length-of-service requirements, law school tenure policies generally include some requirement that the candidate have published a certain number of articles or "units" of scholarship, with definitions of "unit" varying among law schools. If you've written several articles prior to starting, you might be able to negotiate a reduction in the number of articles you're required to produce, although be careful not to frame the issue that way to avoid sending a signal that you don't intend to write much. You might tie it to a request to be considered for tenure on a shorter timeline. Note, though, that faculty members may not fully credit articles written before you were an "accredited" academic with a teaching position. As with credit for service at another school, credit for prior writing is of greater importance to the lateral rather than the entry-level candidate. Moreover, since you likely wrote those articles in stolen moments between other work, you may not be as confident in their quality as articles you will be able to devote more time to. A clean slate might actually benefit you.

DELICATE MATTERS

In the excitement of interviewing and callbacks, it's sometimes difficult to know when to raise ticklish issues, like the fact that your spouse, too, is a law professor or other academic, or has a job that doesn't transplant easily from one part of the country to another. Similarly, as noted in chapter 3, sometimes offers come with ~~strings~~ fuses attached and will "explode" after a certain date. As mentioned earlier, recent years saw an uptick in the number of schools making pre-AALS offers that exploded at the start of the hiring conference.

We discuss here what we euphemistically refer to as "delicate" matters, but understand that these two certainly don't exhaust the universe of such matters. For example, when Denning was interviewing as a lateral candidate for a position with his present law school, the convivial dinner that followed his day of interviews was thrown off course by the revelation that he was due to be awarded tenure in a few weeks, having gone up early. This was news to the hiring chair, who then had to tell Denning that the university prohibited awards of tenure with offers of employment![6] If there is a constant, though, we think it is that there should be open and honest communication between the candidate and the school. Trouble begins, we suspect, when one side senses that the other is not being transparent, or by springing a surprise at the last minute that complicates matters.

---

6. All's well that ends well: Denning gave up tenure to move to his current institution, and went up again after a year, with the understanding that his being awarded tenure at his former institution would be taken into account.

Trailing Spouse

If you have a spouse with a separate career, presumably you have talked over what is involved in looking for an academic job. (In fact, you might want to have him or her read some of the chapters in here, if you sense that he or she doesn't really understand how difficult and contingent this process can be.) At some point, you're going to raise the spouse issue with the schools where you're interviewing, especially if your spouse is an academic or has a specialized job that is not necessarily available everywhere in the country. While our experience is that law schools are eager to help with spousal job searches in any way they can, there is often only so much they can do—especially if the law school is located in a small, medium-sized, or rural locale and your spouse is a commodities trader or an arbitrageur.

As noted in chapter 5, the difficulties are often compounded if your spouse is an academic, and especially if he or she is a law professor. Some faculty members—and we all know a few—have an allergy to hiring spouses. Often the fear—sometimes gendered—is that the "trailing" spouse is going to add little or nothing; that he or she is the price to be paid for getting the "better" half of the couple. Academics who are not law professors might have an even *more* difficult time, since, say, the history department across campus has nothing invested in whether the law school hires this or that candidate, but would object to having a faculty spouse "foisted" on them. They would like to do their own hiring, thank you very much.

As with so much else regarding delicate issues, there are lots of variables to consider that can't be anticipated. That said, we think that open and honest communication between you and the school (and you and your spouse) is the best policy. While your spouse may not be something that you raise initially, gently inquiring about employment opportunities during the callback is appropriate.

Exploding Offers

Most law schools will place some time limit on their offer to you. Naturally, they don't want candidates simply to sit on offers while waiting for a better offer to be made; schools would rather proceed down their list. The longer they wait to do that, the fewer candidates remain. "Exploding offers" are different. The term is usually reserved for an offer with an unreasonably short deadline (say, less than a week); or, more commonly, offers made prior to the Faculty Recruiting Conference that expire the day the Conference begins.[7]

As to the latter, our feeling is that you would have to be convinced to a moral certainty that the law school is the right one for you before accepting such an offer and cancelling all your remaining interviews at the meat market. While we wouldn't say that this could never happen—perhaps you are rooted

---

7. We discussed these briefly in chapter 3. When planning this chapter, Lipshaw's reaction to the AALS's consternation was: "The AALS will say exploding offers are a curse. I, like Tevye, will say, 'Then let God smite me with it, and may I never recover.'"

to a particular area and a law school in that area offers you employment—such occurrences should be regarded as extraordinary.

As for handling deadlines generally, we find that most law school deans actually find it hard to impose rigid deadlines on attractive candidates, especially those who still have callbacks scheduled. Perhaps if the faculty was indifferent as to either of two candidates, but had a mild preference for Candidate A, the dean might limit A so that the school didn't lose B in the bargain if A declined the offer. As with much else, we think communication between the candidate and the dean or the hiring chair is essential. If you think that the timeline is unreasonably short, ask why. Counter with a date by which you think you will be able to let them know. And, if you have multiple callbacks, contact other schools on your list, inform them of the deadline, and see if you can get them to expedite their interviewing or decision-making processes.

HANDLING MULTIPLE OFFERS

If you've got more than one offer, that's great! Sometimes, though, multiple offers can create their own set of problems. For example, perhaps you received an early offer from one school, but your callback to another school (in which you have more interest) is not scheduled until the deadline has expired.[8] How, precisely, you handle this depends on many different variables. A constant, though, is to communicate with all the interested parties, and be open and honest when you do so. No school likes to feel that its offer is being used simply as leverage with other schools; on the other hand, if you're someone the school really wants, they would hate to lose you simply because you have more callbacks to complete.

At a minimum, you should inform the deans at all the schools upon receipt of an offer. You might find that will cause the others to spring into action, perhaps offering to move up your visit to accommodate the deadline. An offer outstanding certainly gives the appointments chair and the dean leverage with the university, if the university must approve visits and is slow in so doing. An offer may also make faculty pay particular attention to a candidate. Think of it like bids at an auction. Sometimes that first offer can move others off the fence.

---

8. Remedying this may not be as easy as moving your callback up. Schools with multiple positions to fill sometimes call back all the candidates in a particular slot and stagger their offers. For example, School A, which is hiring for tax, civil procedure, and criminal law, might invite all the criminal law candidates back first, then the civil procedure folks, then tax. Doing so would allow easy comparison within a subject matter area, but if you're a tax candidate with a particular interest in School A, and School B has given you an offer that expires before you visit School A, you're in a pickle.

SAYING "NO THANKS"

If you are in the enviable position of having more than one offer from your callback schools, then, at some point, you'll have to disappoint someone. This can be difficult. Often there will be a number of faculty members that you really liked, and with whom you established an immediate rapport. But if you've decided that a school isn't for you, and you're going to accept another offer, we think that the right thing to do is to let that school know as soon as possible that they're no longer in the running. It's simply rude to let an offer lapse without so much as a response. And the appointments committee will likely have other candidates on its list; you don't want to disadvantage them in being able to move down their list. Call the dean, the chair of the hiring committee, or both, informing them of your decision. While it is okay, we think, to do this *after* you've formally accepted another school's offer,[9] you should make sure that the other schools hear about your decision from you, and not from a press release or through the academic grapevine. This is a simple matter of accepting the offer, but saying that you'd like to contact the other schools to inform them of your decision. Once that's done, you can notify your new school of that fact and give the dean the go-ahead to announce your hiring publicly.

---

9. The nightmare scenario, which would occur to any lawyer, would be to decline offers from other places, call to accept your offer, and then find that, for whatever reason, it's no longer available. Thus, we think it's okay to accept first, in order to prevent a gap between declining the other offers and accepting the one you want.

CHAPTER SEVEN

Now What? Things to Do Before You Teach Your First Class

Believe it or not, once you have accepted your job, your work *really* begins! In this chapter, we wanted to highlight a few of the most important things that you should do between the time that you accept the offer and the very first time you step in front of a group of students.

SUMMERTIME, AND THE LIVIN' IS ~~EASY~~ CRAZY!

Based on both our own experiences and those of our colleagues in the academy, most new law professors tend to worry about how they will satisfy the scholarship requirements for tenure. While we have some advice on that, the bulk of the advice in this chapter is premised on the fact that the overwhelming majority of stress you will experience during your first year stems from teaching. Planning and executing your courses will consume unimaginable amounts of your time. The more you think and plan on the front end (but not "prep," and there's a difference), the better it will be—and even then you (and your family members) may be surprised to find yourself working longer and harder (though, we hope, happier) than you did in your pre-professor life.

The advice in this chapter proceeds from a few conditions that we think will hold true for most new law professors. First, even if you negotiate a light load (i.e., one class) for your first semester, class preparation will take more time and energy than you ever imagined. Second, as a consequence, you will find it difficult to write during that first semester. Third, as the end of the semester approaches and you plan to use the winter break to catch up on your writing, you are confronted with the realization that you have grading to finish up and *two* additional classes to prepare for in the second semester.

The upshot is that the summer before your first class is time that should be hoarded and spent as economically as possible, since that is likely to be the last substantial block of time that you will have for the rest of the year.

THE LOGISTICS OF TRANSITION

The inestimable value of that summer time means that you should move as soon as feasible, but no later than early summer. While, as noted in chapter 6, you might not be able to begin drawing a salary until the start of the school year, you will likely be able to negotiate a summer research stipend that will allow you to bridge the gap between jobs. If not, we would still advise living frugally your last few months in practice to enable you to live on savings.

Arriving in the summer not only will allow you time to do those little things that make us feel "settled"—familiarize yourself with the town and campus, arrange your office, and so on—but it will be the last completely unencumbered time that you will have for at least the first two years. And believe us when we tell you that you'll need every minute of it, both to prepare for the coming semester and to do some writing.

If you're employed (as opposed to exiting from an LL.M. program, a visiting assistant professorship, or a teaching fellowship) you'll have to notify your current employer of your impending relocation. Again, you will be in the best position to judge when this should occur; but don't assume that concealing it as long as possible is the best course of action. In fact, you will likely want to quit as early as you can afford to in order to have time for all of the work that a move and new job will entail. You'll likely need time to find a place to live, and that may involve more than one trip. If you're up front with your employer, you might be surprised at how much help is forthcoming. In addition, you'll want help winding down existing matters and to alert others that past a certain date, you shouldn't be counted on to begin any new matters. While there would be, no doubt, exceptions, we found our employers extremely understanding—if not downright envious—about our impending departure for the academy!

The AALS New Law Teachers Workshop

As mentioned in earlier chapters, the Association of American Law Schools (AALS) holds a three-day program, usually in the third week of June, usually in Washington, D.C., and sometimes at the same Marriott Wardman Park where you went through the meat market, that is meant to be an orientation for entry-level law professors. Not every session is wonderful, but many are, and it's a great way to build your network of folks in your career cohort. There's also a certain deliciousness in going back to the Wardman Park, if that is where the conference is held, and not interviewing that is, in its own way, quite liberating!

Thinking About Your Course(s)

Since new law professors, by and large, are never taught *how* to teach (except for the couple of hours devoted to it at the AALS New Law Teachers

Workshop), nor do they even necessarily have any teaching experience prior to walking into that first class, there is often very little thought given to what or how to teach. Most simply imitate their mentors, or perhaps use their law school experience as a negative exemplar. But there is much more to effective teaching than imitation or trying *not* to imitate former professors. We would advise new professors to be reflective and purposeful in approaching their first classes. Think about (1) what your goals for the class are; (2) what topics you are going to cover; and (3) how you are going to assess the students.[1]

When thinking about your course(s), it is important to keep in mind that "less is more," particularly the first time through. There will be plenty of time in subsequent years to incorporate the latest teaching technologies, simulations, problems, multiple graded evaluations, and the like. The first time, however, you're going to be better off if you concentrate on the basics: covering the requisite amount of material in an organized, efficient, and timely manner. Even if all you manage to do is get through the syllabus without having to cover 200 pages in the final two days of class, you will likely earn the admiration and appreciation of your students![2]

In doing all of these things, remember that you do not have to reinvent the wheel. New professors should not only call on colleagues in their school, but should also make use of a national network of professors teaching in your field. Don't hesitate to ask for help. Not only will it lighten your load, it will also generate valuable contacts in your specialty. In particular, we have found it helpful to poll colleagues on casebook selection and to solicit syllabi for courses. We discuss each in turn below, though you'll probably be doing these simultaneously. The New Law Professors Section of the AALS maintains a teaching materials network, essentially a list of people willing to share materials,[3] and you may wish to join subject-matter Listservs for access to folks teaching in your area. A number of these are run by the AALS, and your new school's law librarians can help you find more.

---

1. For a great resource on teaching a new course, see Howard E. Katz & Kevin Francis O'Neill, *Strategies and Techniques of Law School Teaching: A Primer for New (and Not So New) Professors* (2009).

2. There's an additional fillip to this. Students know the pecking order. They know if you are a visiting professor, or just starting out, and what strikes you as advanced pedagogy may well seem to them making it up as you go along. Here's a case in point. Lipshaw taught Business Associations out of the Klein, Ramseyer, and Bainbridge casebook as a visitor at Tulane in 2006. He remains convinced to a moral certainty that the subject should be taught as a business-planning course, and not the usual doctrinal procession through agency, partnership, LLC, and corporation. Hence, he rejiggered the casebook order to fit a syllabus that dealt first with an overview of each form, then duties in each form, then management in each form, and so on. A substantial number of the student evaluations clearly indicated a lack of appreciation of the technique. They likely would have reacted differently to the same thing done by a long-term faculty member.

3. Currently, that list is maintained by Susan Rozelle, who is at Stetson University. *See* http://www.law.stetson.edu/teachingmaterialsnetwork/.

Casebook Selection

To continue (or belabor) the family metaphor, once you've accepted a job with a law school and joined the family, the wedding presents arrive: Heavy packages will begin showing up at your door from legal publishers containing every casebook, hornbook, and study aid in the areas you will be teaching. This is lots of fun . . . until they keep coming. There are so many books! How in the world are you going to decide? Eric Muller wrote a very thoughtful article on the subject that we highly recommend you read.[4] We offer this additional advice, as well.

There are at least five common ways new professors pick the wrong book for their style when selecting casebooks. First, there is the tendency simply to choose the book from which you were taught. Second, there is the tendency to go with the most "popular" or most widely adopted book. A third tendency, related to the second, is adopting the book used by your colleagues teaching other sections of the course you will teach. While this may be a good way to ease into a course you do not feel like you have great expertise in, it's easy to feel trapped into that approach in later years even if you don't like the book because of all of the work you invested in that initial class prep. Fourth, some new professors feel obliged to use a book written by a faculty colleague. Finally, some tend to adopt the most theoretically ambitious book. Each of these is a mistake that new professors often come to regret unless they would have picked the book regardless.

As you open your new box of books, it's natural to look first for the book from which you were taught. In fact, you probably *ought* to look at it, even if you don't remember particularly liking it at the time. If nothing else, it may help you recall *why* you didn't like it as a student and help you reflect on what you *are* looking for from other casebooks.

If you're tempted to adopt the book you used, you might ask your old professor whether he or she still uses that book and, if not, what motivated the decision to switch. It may be that the book has weaknesses that were not apparent to you as a student. Even if your professor hasn't switched—inertia is a powerful force—he or she still might recommend a different book.

Sometimes the most popular book, or the one with the widest adoption, is not necessarily the "best" casebook—or, more to the point, the best casebook for *you* and your students. A book may be the most popular only because of the number of professors who default to the book because it was the one out of which they were taught. Another problem is that once-popular casebooks sometimes decline in quality through subsequent editions. There is a tendency among professors to stick with the devil they know, even if said known devil's horns are getting rounded off. This means that inertia and path dependency may drive popularity more than objective merit. Again, asking your colleagues or posting questions to Listservs can alert you to problems.

---

4. Eric L. Muller, *A New Law Teacher's Guide to Choosing a Casebook*, 45 J. Legal Educ. 557 (1995).

Another possible default is to simply use whatever book is used by other professors who teach sections of your course. This can be a mistake, too, and for the reasons already mentioned—the casebook simply isn't a good fit for you, doesn't appeal to your students, or both. So don't feel the need to conform, even if it could garner you a good set of teaching notes![5]

However, there is one situation in which you may find yourself strongly encouraged to conform: where one of your senior colleagues is a casebook *author* and has, ahem, "convinced" her junior (and sometimes senior) colleagues to adopt the book for that course. In that case, you may have to grin and bear it if the casebook isn't particularly good, or risk the displeasure of a colleague.

Finally, resist the temptation to adopt the most theoretically ambitious casebook in your field. This can lead to a dreadful classroom experience with students who, inexplicably, don't live and breathe civil procedure, constitutional law, corporations, contracts, criminal law, legal ethics—whatever it is that consumes your scholarly interest. Sometimes theoretically ambitious casebooks can be very difficult to teach from, even if (sometimes especially if) they contain a wealth of information.[6] Remember that most law school classes are *surveys*. Save the theoretical ambition for advanced classes or for seminars. Use the ambitious casebooks as a reference; many have very good discussion questions or hypotheticals. Some have problems that could be adapted for use on exams. But as you try to get through a class the first few times, we think that a casebook focusing on metatheory is likely to be a hindrance, rather than an aid to effective teaching.

So much for what *not* to do. What criteria should one use to select a good casebook? As we have stressed, some of what makes a good casebook will be entirely a matter of taste—whether you like the look and feel of the book, whether you find it easy to read, and so on. At the same time, we think that as a general rule, you ought to look at the organization, the selection and editing of cases, the notes, and the introductions and transitions in and among sections of the casebook, as well as the overall "voice" of the editor(s). The more that the book approaches the subject the way you would, the better it will likely work for you. Keep in mind that you needn't read books in any detail. You will get a pretty good feel for the book by looking at the table of contents and skimming selections of the readings, a process that will likely take less than half an hour.

Organization

As to organization, even if you have not planned your course in detail, you likely have some opinions as to how the course ought to unfold. If you're

---

5. There is an exception to this rule. Many schools still use the two-semester, six-credit approach to contracts, and some switch teachers midyear. In that instance, there may be a schoolwide standard so that students are not forced to buy two different contracts texts. In those situations, moreover, it is common for the teachers in different sections to consult with each other over the course of the first term as to relative pace.

6. Of one famously theoretical (and famously frustrating for students) casebook, a noted scholar quipped to Denning that it was "a treatise masquerading as a casebook."

teaching contracts, for example, you might have strong opinions about starting with contract formation as opposed to contract remedies. Look at the table of contents of books that you are considering and see if the book's presentation of the material reflects your vision of the course. While you can jump around and reorganize, sometimes material in a casebook is integrated enough to make this more difficult that you might first imagine.

Some of us have additional anecdotal experience that students hate it when the teacher jumps around in the casebook. To keep things as simple as possible for you and your students, you will want to minimize such disruptions as much as possible the first time around.

Case Selection and Editing

Casebook editors have choices about how many cases to include to cover particular topics, and how lightly or heavily to edit the cases. If you are teaching first years, in particular required courses, you may feel it important to choose a casebook that includes canonical cases that are fairly lightly edited, so that students can practice sifting through facts, issues, rules, and holdings and synthesizing rules from multiple sources. On the other hand, if you are teaching upper level courses, you may prefer more heavily edited cases that offer perspective on doctrinal evolution in a particular area. Before assuming that students can read and digest fifty pages a night, it is important to keep in mind—and it is equally easy to forget—that students are taking four or more classes in addition to yours.

Notes

Students often complain about extensive note material in casebooks that poses confusing and unanswerable questions, or asks "questions" followed by case citations that they never look up. Other common complaints are of extensive citations to secondary literature that, again, students will never bother to read. Such extensive scholarly apparatus usually means the casebook in question is one of the metatheory variety described above. On the other hand, judicious use of notes can pose helpful questions that highlight gaps in the case law, or questions left open by doctrine that have gone unanswered by courts. They can also succinctly describe minor cases in doctrinal areas that don't merit reprinting in full. Some casebook editors deliberately eschew all note materials on the theory that if it's important enough, include the case; if not, omit it, because if you stick it in notes students will ignore it.

Introductions, Transitions, and Overviews

We've come a long way from C.C. Langdell's contracts casebook or James Bradley Thayer's constitutional law materials. Earlier casebooks had nothing but cases; newer casebooks not only add "materials," but often include hornbook-like introductions that summarize the topic students are about to study. Students often find such forest-level introductions extremely helpful before they plunge headlong into the trees, uh, cases. Some casebooks, like Eugene Volokh's First Amendment casebook, for example, even begin sections with black-letter outlines. As helpful as such features are for students, don't discount the help that those materials could be to *you* as the first-time teacher!

Casebook "Voice"

If you ask professors why they dislike a particular casebook, you will some-times hear that the casebook was organized in such a way that required them to "teach against" the casebook. For example, if you doubt the utility of eco-nomic analysis in assessing liability under tort law, then you probably won't want to use Richard Epstein's torts casebook. If you are uninterested in what moral philosophy might have to say about legal ethics, then rules-oriented casebooks will probably be better than ones with heavy philosophical con-tent. And so on. Sometimes the casebook authors will be sufficiently well-known that you can predict which way the casebook shades on certain issues. Often—since few consciously prepare an opinionated casebook, lest one nar-row the audience for the book—you'll simply have to compare the treatment of topics among several casebooks.

Teacher's Manuals and Other Support

One of us (Lipshaw) has just completed writing a 350-page teacher's manual for a casebook. The constant refrain among colleagues hearing of that Her-culean effort is that nothing sells a casebook like a good teacher's manual. The upshot is we've done a little thinking on the theory of teacher's manu-als. Teacher's manuals vary in their usefulness. Some are mere afterthoughts. Some are simply one professor's teaching notes. Some are far less concerned with teaching the material than being another source by which the authors can expound on theory that you will never have a chance to cover, and even if you did, the students wouldn't have a clue. Here's a collection of thoughts on the subject in no particular order:

> If you have selected a very problem-oriented casebook, you want a teacher's manual that contains good answers to the problems! It's also a nice touch when the manual contains both the original problem *and* the answer, so that you don't have to keep going back and forth.

> Some manuals have extensive briefs of the cases in the book; some don't. The upside of having the briefs is another check on your own reading of the case; the downside is falling into the habit of not bothering with the case itself!

> The better manuals contain proposed syllabi (see below).

> The best manuals focus not on more theory, but how the authors actu-ally go about teaching the material to average (not gifted) students. This may include hypotheticals not found in the casebook, proposed series of questions and answers to guide your interactive (we won't say Socratic) moments, or group exercises.

> Beware of "manual guilt." Casebooks, particularly those that have now seen many editions come and go, incorporate dozens, if not hundreds, of teacher-years of experience. There is no way that any mere human could

possibly incorporate all of the material into a course and still (1) cover more than one-tenth of the syllabus, (2) speak at a clip of less than 300 words per minute (the normal, by the way, is about 100 to 120 words per minute, and that's in straight lecture), or (3) breathe during the course of a class. Don't feel guilty because you only take 10 or 20 percent of the suggestions offered in the manual!

> Nowadays, casebook authors often provide additional support, particularly in the form of Web sites in which they provide additional materials, most notably PowerPoint or other graphic aids to instruction. While this can simply add another pathology to your already uncontrolled Manual Guilt, for some it's a wonderful resource.

Collecting Syllabi

In addition to syllabi provided in the teachers' manuals, other professors' syllabi are useful for several reasons. First, they allow you to see the coverage choices that professors make in accommodating the credit hours allotted. And even in first-year required courses, choices must be made since many schools have discontinued year-long, six-hour courses in favor of three- or four-hour one-semester courses. Syllabi from your own school also will give you some insight into the amount of reading that you might realistically expect your students to prepare from day to day. In addition, syllabi (especially from your home institution) can be a valuable source of classroom policy "boilerplate" that might not have occurred to you to include. Like contracts, syllabi tend to grow with each passing year, with each new addition representing an unanticipated contingency that required addressing. First it was a reminder to turn cell phones off (or not bring them to class at all); next, we realized we needed an in-class Internet-use policy. The list goes on. Sometimes schools require standardized language on attendance policies or ADA-accommodations policies to be included.

Another great source for syllabi is the AALS New Law Professors Section Teaching Materials Network,[7] which provides contact information for professors who have volunteered to provide materials for new law teachers and is searchable by subject, casebook, and credit hours for the courses available. Some courses may not be covered, and some may have materials for only one casebook or one professor, but many core courses have materials for multiple casebooks and from several professors. It's a great additional resource.

We should note several caveats on syllabi. Pace is highly personal to the teacher. Many teachers will say they emphasize quality over coverage; if they don't make it through the syllabus, that's okay. Be careful. There's a "damned if you do, damned if you don't" problem here. On one hand, if you provide a fulsome syllabus and don't get through it, despite all the caveats in the world about it being a mere approximation, the students will feel like they got cheated out of something. On the other hand, every school has at least one senior professor notorious for going very slowly through material, sprinting

---

7. *Supra* note 3.

through several hundred pages in the remaining three weeks of the semester, then testing heavily on the material she rushed through. This is not a strategy for winning the affection and respect of students. If the reading assignments seem long, be sure to ask the person who provided the syllabus whether she regularly gets through the syllabus, or finds it necessary to omit items or rush through material at the last.[8] And on yet a third hand (if you have one), if you don't provide a syllabus, students will react to the lack of structure and direction (some legendary old-school profs had the following one-sentence syllabus: "Stay fifteen pages ahead of where we are in the reading.")

We strongly recommend that you *not*, when just starting out, try to anticipate the coverage by class period. You are almost guaranteed to fail to correspond to your prediction. Consider putting out a general outline of the topics, but only giving the reading schedule on a month-by-month basis. That leaves you the flexibility of not covering material and not having the students feel like they missed out on something.

Pedagogy and Preparation

One of the most difficult decisions you'll have to make is *how* you plan to teach the course and how you should prepare for each class. For example, do you intend to try to teach by a pure Socratic method? Lecture? Some combination of the two? Before you answer, you should know running a great Socratic dialogue in a class is incredibly difficult—much harder than simply reading a lecture, even if the lectures take more time on the front end to write. Other things to consider: Will you use problems? Assign written work or a midterm?

We won't attempt here to tell you how to teach. Teaching styles, like writing styles, do—and ought to—reflect the person teaching or writing. It will take you a while to find a style with which you're comfortable. You should allow yourself the freedom to experiment, especially your first year, and discard what does not work. Tell your students what your goal is in any particular experiment. They will appreciate understanding what you intend and that you thought about ways to be a better teacher. They can then give better feedback to you. Like writing, teaching is something that has to be *done* in order to improve at it. One does not become a better teacher by reading about teaching alone, any more than reading books about writing alone can improve one's writing.

As to the specifics of preparation, there's the early work and the later work. We do recommend that you spend early preparation time (the summer) before your class reflecting on how you want your classes to run, and thinking about how you can make that come off. Reading through the entire casebook or preparing your full set of class notes during the summer isn't what we're talking about here. Rather, in planning your syllabus and thinking about topics to cover, you should be self-conscious about your objectives for the course. In fact, you should put that in your syllabus. The students will appreciate the

---

8. We know some professors who know that they can finish only a two-credit syllabus in a three-hour class, and that's one strategy as well.

transparency, and it will force you to articulate where you intend to go during the semester. You can repeat this at a micro level, articulating goals for each of the classes that you will meet—the three or four "takeaway points" that you want to leave your students with each day. Having those goals in mind before each class can help keep you on track, and provide a way to introduce and end each class, and a way to segue between classes by reminding the students where you're going, and where you've come from.

Apart from that suggestion, there's no getting around the fact that you will probably have to put in several hours of preparation the first time around for each hour of in-class time. That is to say, if you are teaching three hours a week in the first semester, you can expect at least another nine to fifteen hours of preparation time. If you teach two courses, double it. Even if you *were* to read the casebook through during the summer, you'd have to *reread* the material before you went into class. Eventually the preparation to teaching ratio will even out, but even experienced teachers find it necessary to take an hour or so to prepare for a class, no matter how many times they have taught that class before. It's also a good idea, in that "calming down" period just after class, to jot a few quick notes on what worked and what didn't. You'll use the notes for your prep in a semester or a year, primarily to avoid "déjà vu all over again" on the first-time mistakes.

And how best to prepare? Again, this will be a matter of personal preference. Some new teachers find it comforting essentially to create a "script" for each class with questions and answers—a sort of legal catechism—that can guide Socratic dialogue. Others prefer to create outlines with facts and holdings and ask questions on the fly as class unfolds. Others develop problems and have students work through the hypotheticals. Still others prefer to lecture, especially on technical or arcane subjects and when teaching upper-level students. While we think that some methods are more effective than others, we are not prepared to say that there are absolute "right" and "wrong" ways to teach law students.

But we do stress that the first time through you should strive to keep it simple. Focus on the basics: covering the material in an organized and timely manner. Don't spend all summer on crafting the perfect PowerPoint slides or on creating a really cool role-playing exercise. Those bells and whistles can be added later. Getting through the whole of the semester will be enough work.

Your first semester of teaching is not unlike the first draft of a paper. It will be difficult. It will be messy. You will have to edit extensively. You will doubt yourself and your abilities as a teacher. Our advice is to be prepared to experience all of these emotions, but let yourself off the hook by reminding yourself that this is only your first draft. You will improve.

Looking Ahead

It can be disheartening—if not downright depressing—to realize after that first hard-fought semester draws to a close, you have to begin preparing immediately for *two* (usually) new courses the following semester. Therefore, it is wise to begin the planning early. While we don't recommend spending one's entire summer preparing to teach (see both above and below), there is simply not enough time between the completion of grading the first semester's exams and the start of the second semester to start planning from scratch. Thus, at least a portion of the summer ought to be given over to at least collecting syllabi and winnowing the casebooks for the courses you'll be teaching during your second semester. If you are lucky, perhaps one of the two courses will be a continuation of the first semester. If so, then your workload has just been cut by a third.[9] Other than having more work to do in less time, all you have to do is follow the steps outlined above.

SCHOLARSHIP

As we have throughout, we again stress that this is a *writing* job as much as (or, depending on the school, more than) it is a straight *teaching* gig. Therefore, a substantial chunk of the summer prior to your first semester ought to be devoted to writing. Even if you had published one or more articles before you were hired, and even if you negotiated credit for those articles from your tenure committee, *your new colleagues will breathe a sigh of relief once you write and publish the first article in residence.* It should be a goal to have a manuscript substantially completed at the end of the summer, in time to submit in the fall (even if you hold it until spring). You should also begin planning your second article, even if you don't actually begin to research or write it.

Note that you don't have to turn out your career-making piece in your first summer. Only at the very top law schools is a new professor expected to write paradigm-shifting legal scholarship in her first year. If you wrote a thesis for your LL.M., now's the time to polish it for publication; even if your program didn't have a thesis requirement, you ought to consider turning some of the papers you wrote into articles. Or maybe it's time to finish the article on which your job talk was based. Even a book review essay would be a good summer project.

Why is it so important to get something substantially completed during that first summer? Two reasons: one political, the other practical. The political reason is that it will send a powerful signal to your new colleagues that you are committed to the production of legal scholarship and that you are a self-starter who can get going without having to be told what to do. As we've emphasized elsewhere in this book, because tenure is rarely denied in law schools, and because the nonproductive faculty member is—once tenured—nearly impossible to get rid of, your colleagues will be anxious to see that your hiring was not a mistake! Writing early and often will assuage their concerns on this score.

The second reason is practical: You simply won't have any other time during the first year to get substantial writing done. This fact becomes more

---

9. Note that we didn't say it had been cut by *half.* You've still got to make a syllabus, which involves making all those choices about what to cover, what to omit, how to evaluate, and so on.

likely the greater your outside time commitments (e.g., family). You may have time to do some research, but during the first semester especially, sheer panic will likely lead you to devote most of your nonclass time to preparing for your next class. As the semester draws to a close, you will be writing exams; during the holidays, you'll be grading them. After you finish grading, you'll probably go to the AALS annual convention, and then midway through the convention, you'll begin panicking about the fact that you have those two additional classes to teach right when you get back. And so on.

There is another practical reason to get the first article as a new faculty member under your belt, and that's the relief *you* will feel at having gotten it finished. This relief can produce a feeling of confidence that, in turn, can result in a certain amount of momentum that could carry you through your next piece or two. On the other hand, we've all seen colleagues who, for whatever reason, didn't complete the first article that first year. Some find themselves blocked as a result, succumb to the temptation to procrastinate, and end up desperately writing as the promotion or tenure clock begins to run out. And after your first year, when you begin to assume committee duties, find yourself advising students and student groups, and so on, you will have numerous excuses for continuing to procrastinate.

CONCLUSION: THE IMPORTANCE OF TIME MANAGEMENT

We'll say it again: You will be very busy during your first year. It will surprise you how exhausting preparing for and teaching class will be. The summer prior to your first class offers both an opportunity and something of a last chance to have a large block of otherwise unoccupied time to think and write. Use it wisely. It will be a good opportunity to practice time management skills that are essential to keeping your head in the hectic academic year to come. Keep in mind that you are likely used to having externally imposed deadlines that served as your primary motivation, whether it was a due date for a school assignment or a filing deadline in practice. You will not have those anymore, so you'll have to come up with a new system of internal deadlines or some other workable motivation strategy. Whatever works for you—making to-do lists, assigning specific tasks to specific days, even trying to allocate hours within each day to tasks on your list—you should put it into practice, lest the summer slip away with little to show for it but a daunting list of things that you had intended to get done and a lingering sense of regret that none of them are marked off! Finally, resist the urge to physical violence that will come over you when friends and former colleagues comment on what a nice job you have that only requires you to "work" three or six hours a week and gives you your summers "off."

CHAPTER EIGHT

Converting an Unsuccessful Job Search into Future Opportunities

This is the chapter that we hope that you don't have to reread. But as we explain below, not getting callbacks or offers does not mean the end of your dream of being a law professor. There are any number of reasons beyond your control that might contribute to your not receiving offers of employment. We start with those reasons, because it's important that you not interpret a failure to get an offer as a judgment on your future employment prospects. We then discuss ways that you can attempt to learn from this year's experience, and how you can use your time to maximize your chances the next (or in future) years. The message of this chapter is simple: Be patient and continue to write and publish.

WHY DIDN'T YOU GET AN OFFER (OR CALLBACKS)?

Failure to receive an offer or callbacks can be incredibly discouraging. Some candidates assume that getting into law teaching won't ever happen for them, and either return to practice, or find something else to do. Those are certainly options, but if you're still attracted to being an academic, you should hang in there, not beat yourself up, and make whatever adjustments are within your control in anticipation of the next hiring cycle.

It's not all that unusual to go through the cycle more than once; that happened to all of us as well as to a number of famous professors teaching at super-elite schools. Remember, only about 15 percent of the applicants in any given Faculty Recruitment Conference (FRC) pool are getting jobs that year. While it's possible there's something irreparably disqualifying about you, the fact is that many highly qualified candidates aren't getting callbacks or offers either. For example, there was a significant blemish on Lipshaw's resume: He had spent far too long in practice, getting far too much experience. He had ten interviews at the 2005 FRC, nine of which, by his estimation, went about as well as could be expected, but he did not get a single callback. A year later, he had thirteen interviews, and seven callbacks. He's pretty sure two things helped:

(1) He had the fortuity of being offered, and taking, despite having to commute during his son's senior year in high school, a visiting professorship at Tulane for the 2006–07 year (as the school was recovering from the effects of Hurricane Katrina on the faculty), and (2) figuring out that the tale of his particular sojourn from practice to teaching shouldn't consume any more than about three minutes of the FRC interview.

We discuss some of the other adjustments below, but we want to start by saying that your failure to get hired may be due to factors that were or continue to be completely *outside* your control.

> *Budget issues.* As we write this, the country is in a severe economic downturn whose duration is uncertain. All schools have suffered a decrease in endowment money; state schools face the additional hit of budget cuts from state governments. As a result, institutions of higher education—public and private—are looking to reduce expenditures however they can. Given that faculty salaries often constitute the largest budget line-item at law schools, not hiring when you don't absolutely have to is an easy way to save money.

> *Curricular needs.* Some schools' searches, especially in hard times, are largely or entirely curriculum-driven. Priorities sometimes shift as the search progresses; sometimes committees encounter unanticipated resistance by the rest of the faculty, or a surprising intensity of preference for filling certain needs. Occasionally, unexpected vacancies suddenly cause the focus of a committee to shift. A variation on the curriculum-driven search is a fad-driven search. Committees are susceptible to feeling they need to hire someone in a "hot field" or students won't attend their law school. Over the years, we've seen the following hot fields bid up the currency of candidates who want to teach in them: environmental law, health law, intellectual property, international and comparative law, and transactional law. If you happen to go on the market in a year when your field is the hot one, you'll reap the benefits—more interviews, and interviews at higher-ranked schools as well. On the other hand, if you're "criminal law/criminal procedure" the year everyone is looking for public international law folks, then you might experience the reverse.

> *Faculty/university politics.* Especially in these trying economic times, law school hiring plans will encounter resistance from their host universities. Sometimes this resistance manifests itself only *after* candidates have been interviewed and, in some cases, after preliminary approval to hire has already been given. Sometimes within law school faculties, objections will be made to the course of the hiring process—either objections to the candidates themselves or to the curricular focus of the hiring process. In neither case will it be under your control.

> *Diversity pressure.* Whatever your feelings about taking race, gender, and ethnicity into account when hiring, it happens. Faculties on which older, white males are overrepresented often face pressure from the Association of American Law Schools (AALS), their host university, and sometimes from students and faculty to diversify the faculty. If you happen

to be white, you might be edged out if racial or ethnic diversity is a goal of hiring. Likewise, if you happen to be male, you might be edged out if gender diversity is a goal that year. That said, do not assume that is the only factor if you fail to get a job. It likely was not the sole factor and it's something about you that you cannot change, so focusing on it does no one much good.

> *Competitive market.* The legal academic market varies in size and overall quality of candidates from year to year. In some years, it is a seller's market, with fewer qualified candidates being chased by more schools with multiple hires to make that year. Conversely, in other years, you might have more excellently credentialed candidates chasing fewer jobs because fewer schools are hiring for fewer positions. Thus, a candidate who might have been highly sought after in one year may have few interviews and no offers in another year simply because of the competition.

> *Entry-level versus lateral hires.* Occasionally law schools will interview both entry-level candidates and promising lateral candidates from other law schools for the same position(s). It might be that the law school decided to go with a lateral candidate, and not hire any entry-levels that particular year. Laterals with both a record of publication as well as teaching experience are sometimes seen as a lesser risk for schools with limited hires to make. On the other hand, laterals are often more expensive than entry-level hires.

See, there are lots of reasons that have nothing to do with *you* that could explain why you might not be hired the first year you go on the market! Since you probably won't know which applied to you, we encourage you to choose any of the ones we listed, if it will enable you to dust yourself off and prepare for the next hiring cycle.

However, even if the reasons given are "it's-not-you-it's-me" reasons, there is the possibility that something happened at the interview or the callback that convinced faculty that you were not a great fit with their institution. If you think that might be the case—and absent a really horrible visit, you probably won't—you might consider asking for feedback after receiving the letter indicating that you didn't get the job. But this is a matter requiring both a thick skin and a light touch on your part.

CONSIDER ASKING FOR FEEDBACK

The first question that you need to ask is whether you are really interested in a frank assessment of your performance at a particular school. This is not a question with an obvious answer. If you can self-evaluate, and pinpoint areas of improvement yourself, then there's probably no need to have that self-critique confirmed by others. You might get discouraged or disheartened, especially if the criticism is frank to the point of being brutal.

If you would like feedback, how do you go about getting it? Assuming that you are most interested in feedback from schools in which you had a particular interest or at which you thought you had a particularly good shot at being hired, we recommend that you e-mail your faculty shepherd and ask whether she might be able to give you feedback about your visit on things within your control that you might improve upon for next year. We want to emphasize two things: (1) Send an e-mail instead of calling. A call with that request would likely put the person on the spot. (2) Stress that you're not looking for inside information about faculty deliberations and the like. You're asking specifically about things under your control that might have affected your chances.

It's possible that you won't hear anything at all, or your contact will profess not to have anything helpful to offer. While your contact might simply be equivocating, it is just as likely that your failure to get an offer can be chalked up to the forces beyond your control described above. If, on the other hand, your contact does have some critiques of your performance, please take them in the spirit in which they are offered. Don't become defensive. The person is doing you a service of inestimable value if you intend to go back on the market in the future. And, frankly, it is almost as difficult to *give* constructive criticism as it is to hear constructive criticism. If the critique is vague, ask questions; the more specific the criticisms are, the more helpful they are to you. Take good notes and try to formulate a to-do list based on the feedback; if the criticism was upsetting to you, wait a few days before making your list, when emotions are less raw. Commonly, criticisms focus on the job talk or on the paper on which it was based. The other—and admittedly less helpful comment—will be a sense among the faculty that there isn't a good "fit" between the candidate and the existing faculty. The latter, however, is of a piece with the "it's-not-you-it's-me" reasons over which you have very little control.

CONTINUE TO WRITE AND NETWORK

The most important thing to do is to continue to write and publish even if you didn't luck out on the job market the first time. Adding lines to your list of publications can never hurt; it will continue to send the signal that you are serious about your candidacy and that you are motivated.

In addition to writing, consider ways in which you might network with other legal academics who might be serving on appointments committees in the years to come. One way is to attend conferences and workshops in your areas of interest. If you are still in practice, you might use such conferences as an opportunity to satisfy your continuing legal education requirements. A list of conferences, symposia, and calls for papers can be found on a blog maintained by faculty and staff at the University of Pittsburgh and the University of Washington.[1] Be subtle. Let folks know that you are planning to go on the

---

1. LEGAL SCHOLARSHIP BLOG, http://legalscholarshipblog.com/ (last visited Mar. 27, 2009).

market, but don't constantly press them for information about hiring at their schools or thrust your CV on them at every turn. Rather, cultivate these relationships in an effort to be part of the scholarly conversation in your chosen area. Read the scholarship of others and offer your comments if they are interested or ask questions that will shed light on your own work. Ask them to do the same. If you network with a light touch, your name will float to the top without too much additional effort on your part.

CHECK OUT THE COMPETITION

As we've noted several times, Illinois law professor Larry Solum collects data about entry-level hires on his *Legal Theory Blog*.[2] He lists schools, their hires, and basic education information about entry-level hires. It might be helpful to see just *who* exactly got hired, if you did not have any luck. By looking at their backgrounds, you might be able to ascertain whether there was a hot field that year, whether the competition was particularly fierce, or whether there were lots or only a few law schools hiring. With a little work, you can find out more about the successful candidates and compare their CVs with yours.

APPLY FOR VAPS OR LL.M. PROGRAMS

VAPs and Fellowships

We described visiting assistant professorships (VAPs) and fellowships in some detail in chapter 2, but in general, these are temporary positions designed to give candidates teaching experience and time to write prior to going on the market for a tenure-track job. These programs offer a hedging opportunity for candidates, and you should start collecting information on these programs about the time you submit your FAR form (see chapter 3) to the AALS, lest you miss deadlines. Paul Caron maintains a list of fellowships and VAP programs with links to the sponsoring institutions on his *TaxProf Blog*.[3]

A VAP or a fellowship would be a very good "second best" outcome if a tenure-track position is not forthcoming. Not only would there be—in theory—extra time to write, VAPs and even some fellowships offer the opportunity to get valuable teaching experience. You would also have a ready audience with whom to practice your job talk, hone your interviewing skills, and who could review drafts and generally offer advice and guidance. On the other hand, if you have a family and a working spouse, the costs involved in possibly making two or more moves before you land a permanent position can be prohibitive.

---

2. LEGAL THEORY BLOG, http://lsolum.typepad.com/legaltheory/.

3. See TAXPROF BLOG, *Fellowships for Aspiring Law Professors*, http://taxprof.typepad .com/taxprof_blog/2010/08/Fellowships-For-Aspiring.html (updated Aug. 31, 2010.)

LL.M. or S.J.D. Programs

If you don't already have an advanced law degree, you might investigate these opportunities in an effort to become what we called the Revised Standard Model Candidate. All of the caveats from chapter 2 apply. Not all LL.M. programs are created equal, and, if you have an LL.M. already, getting the S.J.D. may not enhance your marketability appreciably. On the other hand, it does demonstrate a commitment to the process, and both programs—especially the S.J.D., where a substantial thesis will be required—hold out the possibility of enabling you to write. Like VAPs, though, these can be costly for all the reasons discussed previously.

***

We want to emphasize what we said at the beginning of the chapter. Your failure to get a job the first time through is not the end of your dream of being a law professor. All of us were repeat visitors to the FRC. Lack of success the first time through certainly does not signify a personal failing on your part. As we've said throughout this book, one often has to be good *and* lucky to succeed in the job lottery. Be patient. Make whatever adjustments you can. Continue networking, and continue writing.

***

We hope this book has helped you see that if you want to become a law professor, with enough hard work, you probably can. The key, as with any career, is doing the right kind of work, being persistent, and seizing the opportunities to make your own luck along the way.

Bibliographic Essay

We began this book, in part, because there *wasn't* much published about entering the job market, what schools were looking for, and so on. A bit more is available than was the case when we began this book almost four years ago. Much of it, however, comes in blog postings that are somewhat ephemeral. Instead of attempting an exhaustive bibliography, we highlight here what we have found to be the most helpful—and most accessible—pieces of advice about getting hired in the legal academy.

BOOKS

Ronald Eades's book *How to Be a Law Professor Guide: From Getting That First Job To Retirement* (2008) covers some of the same ground that we do, but in less detail. Professor Eades's book has a broader scope, offering advice to law professors at all stages of their career. Similarly, Howard E. Katz & Kevin Francis O'Neill, *Strategies and Techniques of Law School Teaching* (2009), and Madeleine Schachter's *The Law Professor's Handbook: A Practical Guide to Teaching Law Students* (2003), both offer tips and suggestions for structuring and teaching classes in much greater detail than we offer in chapter 7. (For an extremely useful bibliography on law teaching generally, see Mary Olszewska & Thomas E. Baker, *An Annotated Bibliography on Law Teaching*, http://papers.ssrn.com/sol3/papers.cfm?abstract_id=1497031.)

ARTICLES

Several older articles described the way in which law professors are hired in the United States. Of particular interest is William L. Prosser, *Advice to the Lovelorn*, 3 J. LEGAL ED. 505 (1951), which offers some historical perspective on the hiring process. (Dean Prosser laments how many candidates want to teach constitutional and administrative law, and how difficult it is to find good criminal or commercial law teachers! *Plus ça change. . . .*) James Gordley, *Mere Brilliance: The Recruitment of Law Professors in the United States*, 41 AM. J. COMP. L. 367 (1993), draws on the author's experience as a member of his school's (U.C.-Berkeley) hiring committee and discusses what he finds essential in a strong candidate for teaching. When you fill out your FAR form, you will also receive a copy of Don Zillman et al., *Uncloaking Law School Hiring: A Recruit's Guide to the AALS Faculty Recruitment Conference*, 38 J. LEGAL ED. 345 (1988). Denning recalls reading it so many times he had it practically memorized, but wished it was longer. Another interesting take on the state of the profession circa 1988 can be found in Frank T. Read & M. C. Mirow, *So Now You're a Law Professor: A Letter from the Dean*, 2009 CARDOZO L. REV. DE NOVO 55, available at http:www.cardozolawreview .com/index.php?option=com_content&view=article&id=107:mirow200955. The letter was written to Professor Mirow from his Dean when he accepted his first teaching job. It is reproduced with Professor Mirow's observations on the current state of the academy in the footnotes.

More recent articles include Jack Chin and the late Denise Morgan's *Breaking into the Academy:* The Michigan Journal of Race & Law's 2002–2004 *Guide for Aspiring Law Professors*, 7 MICH. J. RACE & L. 457 (2002), which has a number of very helpful short articles written by a number of distinguished authors. Debra R. Cohen, *Matchmaker, Matchmaker, Make Me a Match: An Insider's Guide to the Faculty Hiring Process*, http://ssrn.com/abstract=931995, analogizes the process to Internet dating and is based on her interviews with and mentoring of scores of candidates over the years. Another humorous look at the process is Kevin H. Smith, *How to Become a Law Professor Without Really Trying: A Critical, Heuristic, Deconstructionist, and Hermeneutical Exploration of Avoiding the Drudgery Associated with Actually Working as an Attorney*, 47 U. KAN. L. REV. 139 (1998). Read it with care, however, as the article's distinction between scholarship-oriented and teaching-oriented schools is now dated. The advice offered on how to prepare for the job talk, moreover, would be a recipe for disaster if taken seriously. If you're looking for more advice about the job talk, look for the forthcoming essay from Anne Enquist, Paula Lustbader & John B. Mitchell, *From Both Sides Now: The Job Talk's Role in Matching Candidates with Law Schools* (copy on file with authors). Not only does it contain advice for the candidate, it is also a call for schools to be more thoughtful about what purpose, exactly, the job talk serves in the hiring process.

Every candidate ought to read David Case's personal account of his twelve-year odyssey, and ask themselves whether, if they knew that's how long it might take, they would still take the plunge. David W. Case, *The Pedagogical Don Quixote de la Mississippi*, 33 U. MEM. L. REV. 529 (2003). And of course, Jeffrey L. Lipshaw, *Memo to Lawyers: How Not to Retire and Teach*, 30 N.C.CENT. L. REV. 151 (2008), is essential reading for those with considerable practice experience who are contemplating filling out an FAR. For some empirical information on recent hires, see Richard E. Redding, *Where Did You Go to Law School? Gatekeeping for the Professoriate and Its Implications for Legal Education*, 53 J. LEGAL ED. 594 (2003). Finally, Michael Asimow has a brief summary of the hiring process for those interested in teaching administrative law in *How to Get a Job Teaching Administrative Law*, in CAREERS IN ADMINISTRATIVE LAW AND REGULATORY PRACTICE (James T. O'Reilly ed.,

2010), also published by the ABA's Section of Administrative Law and Regulatory Practice. And though you probably won't need to worry about lateraling to another law school anytime soon, Paul M. Secunda, *Tales of a Law Professor Lateral Nothing*, 39 U. MEM. L. REV. 125 (2008), is a great primer on how to move from one job to another.

INTERNET ARTICLES AND BLOGS

In addition to the books and articles above, several professors have offered their thoughts on the law school hiring process. Brian Leiter and Brad Wendel's essays are excellent examples; both are must-reads for prospective candidates.

> Brian Leiter, *Information and Advice for Persons Interested in Teaching Law* (Aug. 2009), http://www.law.uchicago.edu/alumni/careerservices/academicjobsearch.

> Brad Wendel, *The Big Rock Candy Mountain: How to Get a Job in Law Teaching* (last updated Oct. 29, 2009), http://ww3.lawschool.cornell.edu/faculty-pages/wendel/teaching.htm. Brad's essay is chock full of helpful links to blog posts and other articles on the Web.

Around the time hiring season begins to kick-off, many habitués of the popular group law blogs, like *The Volokh Conspiracy, Concurring Opinions, Prawfsblawg,* and *The Faculty Lounge,* will weigh in with advice, observations, and predictions. We might advise you, however, not to read the comment section during this time, as candidates who do report experiencing shortness of breath, arrhythmia, sweating, and other stress-related symptoms associated with reading some anonymous commenter's lament that he or she has "only" seventeen interviews and is considering not going to the conference.

A Primer on Law Review Submissions

Given the importance of writing to landing a law teaching job, it is imperative to understand how, precisely, one gets published. We wanted to include a
brief account of the process in our book, though legal writing and law review
submissions could—and do—constitute a subject for a separate book and
some great articles.[1] We describe the process for submitting to the standard,
student-edited law reviews first, then take up some particular questions at the
end.

SUBMISSION SEASON

In general, one submits articles to law reviews in either the spring or the fall.
Spring submission season now begins as early as late February, when law
review editorial boards turn over and the new board begins to fill the allotted
books in its volume. The spring season generally runs until the end of April
or the first of May, when students begin studying for exams. The fall submissions season begins in late August, as students return to school. Remaining
books are usually filled by October or early November.

It is a matter of some debate whether it is better to submit in the fall or
the spring. One school of thought holds that spring is better because there
are more open spots: New boards are starting with a clean slate. In the fall,
by contrast, not only have a good number of spots been filled the previous
spring, but there are more manuscripts chasing the remaining spots, as professors have used the summer to complete projects.

It is possible to place articles outside the two submission seasons
described here. Specialty journals sometimes accept "off-season" submissions; and general law reviews sometimes find themselves with space to fill.

---

1. For more information, see, for example, Eugene Volokh, *Academic Legal Writing: Law
Review Articles, Student Notes, Seminar Papers, and Getting on Law Review* (3d ed. 2007);
Leah M. Christensen & Julie Oseid, *Navigating the Law Review Article Selection Process:
An Empirical Study of Those With All the Power—Student Editors*, 59 S.C. L. REV. 465
(2008); Nancy Levit & Allen Rostron, *Information for Submitting Articles to Law Reviews &
Journals*, http://papers.ssrn.com/sol3/papers.cfm?abstract_id=1019029.

A few journals have special summer submissions processes.[2] If you have an article ready to go outside the ordinary submissions cycles, you might try submitting it to a few law reviews to see what happens, but do so knowing that most offers are made during the fall or the spring seasons. That said, you have little to lose in trying to submit; at worse, you'll have to submit it again in the next cycle. You might contact law reviews directly and ask if they are still considering manuscripts.

FORMATTING YOUR DRAFT FOR SUBMISSION

Some law reviews try to have something like blind review for article selection, and so ask that you submit your article without any identifying information in it, but not all reviews do so and in fact prefer to have the author information to more easily keep track of submissions. An easy way to comply with both preferences is to include a cover page as the article's first page. That page might contain just the title, your name, and if you include one, your asterisk footnote identifying yourself and giving any thanks you need to. The first page of text, then, would contain only the title. That way, reviews can easily exclude that page, giving reviewers only the rest of the article to review.

Moreover, contemporary word processing programs are now such that you can make your drafts look almost exactly like they would once published in a print law review. Law review templates, like the one from the University of California-Davis (http://office.microsoft.com/en-us/templates/TC300002991033.aspx?ofcresset=1) can be downloaded and used to format your draft to look exactly like a "real" law review article.

Is using a template like this worth the effort? Does it make a difference to law review editors? We don't know. A professor-friend at an elite school reported back to one of us the law review editor was "impressed" with the fact that it was in the above template form. (That said, it did not engender an offer.) Individually, we have spent a lot of (too much) effort to make the drafts look pretty, only to garner not a single offer. On the other hand, we know of people who write their drafts in nothing but 12-point, double-spaced, Courier font, who have had articles published in the *Harvard Law Review.* If you decide not to spend time formatting your drafts in this way, we doubt seriously that your manuscript will be at any material disadvantage.

---

2. In the summer submission processes, you submit to that journal, sometimes exclusively, and you get a response fairly quickly. By submitting during the summer, you agree to accept an offer if it is made. Alabama and Washington & Lee have done this in the past, but programs change from year to year, so we suggest that you do a search when you are ready, perhaps with the terms "law review summer submission."

POSTING DRAFTS ON SSRN

If your draft is ready to submit to law reviews, then it's likely ready for posting on SSRN. Posting on SSRN can garner you some publicity—folks see your article and e-mail you or blog about it. It is also a handy place to refer prospective employers wishing to see a sample of your work. Several years ago some law reviews took the position that posting on SSRN was "publication" and either would make authors take the paper down once it was being edited, or would not consider it at all. Thankfully, no general law review now seems to take that position. Many publication agreements, in fact, permit the posting of papers on SSRN or on an author's Web site.

SUBMISSION MECHANICS

Most general and specialty law reviews accept electronic submissions now; in fact, many prefer them. There are at least two services that permit you to submit to multiple law reviews electronically: ExpressO (http://law.bepress.com/expresso/) and LexOpus (https://lawlib.wlu.edu/lexopus/index.aspxy). LexOpus, which was started by a law librarian at Washington and Lee University, submits manuscripts to law reviews twenty at a time, adding additional journals as rejections come in. ExpressO, on the other hand, allows authors to submit simultaneously to as many journals as they wish, and to update the submissions to other reviews as rejections come in. Note that ExpressO has a larger number of U.S. law journals participating. ExpressO also charges a fee for the delivery of each manuscript, but many schools have institutional accounts with generous credits for each submission. (If you aren't submitting an article as a visiting assistant professor (VAP) or as part of a fellowship program, you might ask your law school alma mater if you could submit on its account, explaining that this is part of your master plan to become a law professor. Once again, it never hurts to ask.)

A number of the elite law reviews (Harvard, Yale, Stanford, Penn, Columbia, etc.) have their own electronic submissions process that they prefer submitters to use. If you want to submit to these journals, then you'll have to submit separately to each one, in addition to the general ExpressO or LexOpus submission. While this takes some time, the school-specific submission process is free.

In addition to the copy of your paper that you upload, many journals request that you upload a copy of your CV and a cover letter. The cover letter gives you a chance to explain concisely the contribution that your piece makes to the literature, so you want to take a bit of time to sell the piece. Don't simply summarize the article, although a short summary is a good idea. Instead, give the context—why did you want to write it; why hasn't anyone else yet; why will scholars, courts, and practitioners find it useful? Many reviews also require you to include a word count for the paper in your cover letter, both the total words (including footnotes) and just the text. This makes it easy for those law reviews that distinguish between "essays" and "articles" based on word count to categorize the piece, and it also ensures that you have complied with any absolute limitations that journals impose.[3]

SUBMISSION STRATEGY

Just as *U.S. News & World Report* ranks law schools, a number of people rank law journals. Some rankings, for example, ExpressO's ranking of general journals, mirror the *U.S. News* rankings, but some do not. LexOpus ranks journals by "impact factor," that is, how many times articles are cited in other works, and by "currency factor," that is, how quickly they're cited. Some specialty journals are ranked higher than general journals in this system, whereas other systems place specialty journals in a special categories.

If you talk to ten different law professors, you are likely to get at least five different approaches to submitting to law reviews. Some submit to the top 100 law reviews and accept the first offer they receive. Others argue that it's better to stagger submissions—to submit to journals ranked 51–100 first, then a couple of weeks later submit to the top 50. The theory is that the two week stagger gives an opportunity to get an offer from a lower-ranked journal that can be used to seek expedited review (see below) from those that are ranked higher and to give an impression that the piece is "hot." Still others don't stagger, simply submitting to the top 50 or 100 journals, see if any offers are forthcoming, and then play the expedited review game or not, depending on how good the initial offer is.

Because it can be difficult as someone *not* currently on faculty somewhere[4] to get *any* offer, we don't think that you need be as choosy as you might become once you've been hired. As a prospective candidate, we think that you can be a little less concerned about the rank of the law review with which you publish. This is not to say that you should be completely indifferent, but neither is it true that schools will only find it impressive that you published in one of the twenty-five or thirty "top twenty" law reviews, unless you have your sights set on the elite law schools.

---

3. Responding to criticisms that articles were getting too long to be useful, a growing number of journals refuse to consider pieces that contain more than a certain number of words or strongly encourage authors to limit the length of their articles. Typical limitations are 25,000 to 35,000 words including footnotes. *See* Daniel Solove, *Law Review Article Submission Resources* (Spring 2008), CONCURRING OPINIONS (Feb. 21, 2008), http://www.concurringopinions.com/archives/2008/02/law_review_arti_7.html#more-12011.

4. This difficulty would be another reason that you might find VAPs or fellowships particularly useful.

OFFERS

If all goes well, you'll receive some expressions of interest from law reviews within four to six weeks of submission—sometimes it takes longer, though, depending on how many submissions the review is wading through. You'll get either a call or an e-mail from the editor. Usually this offer is accompanied by an expiration date. Our sense is that the length of time between offer and expiration has shrunk over time, as many law reviews have tried to resist authors' attempts to use their offers as stalking horses for offers from other law reviews. In general, though, two weeks is not unreasonable. Sometimes you can even extend a time limit that is about to expire. It is during this time that you will want to request expedited review from other law reviews.

THE ETIQUETTE AND ETHICS
OF EXPEDITED REVIEW

Once you get an acceptable offer (and we'd advise you not to submit to any journal from which you would not accept one), you are in the money, and ready to start the expediting game. As with job offers, nothing makes you popular like being popular: The best evidence to many student editors that something is worthy of publication is that it got another offer. Almost all law reviews therefore have an "expedited review" mechanism whereby they will accelerate their review and decision if you have another offer pending.

As is true for original submissions—we remember having to photocopy and mail manuscripts individually—technology has made this process easier. On ExpressO's site, for example, you can request expedited review by e-mail simply by checking boxes and sending a mass e-mail. Reviews from which you're requesting expedited review will all want to know at least the name of the journal from which you received the offer, and the date by which you have to let that journal know. Strategies again vary, with some authors expediting from the next "tier" of law reviews (if you got an offer from law review number 50, you would expedite with numbers 49–25), in hoping of obtaining other, higher offers that can in turn be "walked up" the rankings. Others simply pick higher-ranked law reviews with which they'd rather publish and expedite with those. Don't worry about requesting time to shop the piece around—law review editors are sophisticated; they know the deal and expect that authors will do this.

If you're fortunate enough to receive multiple offers, we think that it's just good manners to cut one or more reviews loose by withdrawing the piece, even if you are still trying to expedite with other reviews. Similarly, we think it is polite to send withdrawals if you have a single offer you would accept—but for the expediting—to any journals to which you do not send the expediting request.[5] As with the original submission, we think that you ought not expedite with any journal in which you would not, at the end of the day, publish.

ACCEPTANCE—AT LAST!

Eventually, you hope, you'll be able to accept some offer. You'll be asked to sign a publication agreement, which have become mercifully simpler over time. You should also receive some kind of production schedule. Note that the law review will likely move more slowly than you would like it. This is less of a problem these days, because of your ability to post your manuscript on SSRN and indicate where it is forthcoming.

SPECIAL ISSUES

Here are a few perennial questions that come up when law reviews and submissions to law reviews are discussed.

Student-Edited Versus Peer Review

As you know, the overwhelming majority of law reviews in the United States are student-edited. The students select the articles and oversee the editing. This is not the case with other academic journals in the United States or with law journals in other countries, which are peer-reviewed, meaning that the articles are selected by boards of editors who are experts in the field. This is not the place to rehash the arguments for and against peer-reviewed journals, but know that there are some peer-reviewed law journals (examples include the *Journal of Legal Studies*, *Constitutional Commentary*, and the *Journal of Empirical Legal Studies*), and publication in peer-reviewed journals, if that journal is well known, is considered more prestigious and a more reliable signal of an article's quality than publication in a student-edited law journal. Some peer-reviewed journals are not well known outside of the particular field. Additionally, some elite journals, like the *Stanford Law Review* and the *Harvard Law Review*, currently engage in a form of peer review, where articles under consideration will be circulated for comment to outside experts. Other law reviews like the *South Carolina Law Review* are also experimenting with peer review, but it is not currently the norm.

Along with being more prestigious, publication in a peer-reviewed journal is more difficult, and can take considerably longer than publication with a general journal, first because you are generally required to submit exclusively to the journal (because you are taking up the time of professors, not just

---

5. ExpressO makes withdrawing articles easy, too. You need only check the law reviews from which you wish to withdraw your submission and a customizable e-mail is generated and then sent to those law reviews you selected.

students), and second, because the review process itself can take months or even years. Unless you have done some specialized work in, say, legal history or some very good empirical work that you think student-edited journals are unlikely to be able to evaluate or appreciate, we would counsel sticking with the student-edited journals as you try to get a teaching job.

There is one other consideration in deciding whether to go "peer-reviewed." Most peer review is "double-blind"; that is, you don't know who the reviewers are, and they don't know who you are. If your work is exceptionally good, you have a leg up when the reviewers don't know that you are a mere entrant to the field. Moreover, if you do not have a Ph.D. in another discipline (like economics or philosophy), but your work is cross-disciplinary in those fields, acceptance in a peer-reviewed journal after blind review is a validation that you indeed have something to contribute to the field. One of the reasons we think many law professors don't contribute to peer-reviewed journals (in addition to exclusive submission and the length of time) is that, unlike law review editors, peer reviewers actually comment on the work, often with the conclusion "revise and resubmit," or worse, "I cannot recommend this piece for publication." We confess that some of our worst moments in academia have come while reading the scathing commentary of some unknown professor panning the very idea of the essay we submitted.

General Journals Versus Specialty Journals

Another subject that can always generate debate is whether you're better off publishing in a general law review or a specialty law review. The question is usually framed this way: Would you rather publish in a flagship state university law school's general law review or in an elite law school's specialty journal? The answer, as you might guess, is that it depends. In some cases, specialty journals (those in tax, for example) are closely read by experts in that field. Publishing in them would be a way to get your name known and to attract attention. On the other hand, others not familiar with the specialty might not know which specialty journals are must-reads in particular fields. All things being equal, we think it is probably better to go with the reputation of the school, especially when you're just starting out.

From Resume to CV

"Before": sample resume as constructed by professional executive recruiter for the corporate and law firm world.

Jeffrey M. Lipshaw

[Contact Information]

PROFESSIONAL EXPERIENCE

Counsel to Board of Directors of Fortune 850, NYSE-traded company

> Advised the Board of Directors of Great Lakes Chemical Corporation regarding, and directed the legal activity for, its merger with Crompton Corporation (to form Chemtura Corporation)
> Sarbanes-Oxley and NYSE compliance and corporate governance
>> *Corporate Secretary* magazine "Corporate Governance Top 10 Most Improved," April/May 2003
>> GovernanceMetrics International: "10" corporate governance rating for 2003 (one of the 22 out of 2,100 companies worldwide)
>> Ranked as high as 7th in CGQ (Corporate Governance Quotient) for S&P 500 firms per Institutional Shareholder Services
> Take-over defense strategy and shareholder resolutions
> Directors' and officers' insurance

Corporate, mergers & acquisitions and securities counsel in-house and in private practice

> $1.5 billion sale of multinational automotive brake business (AlliedSignal, Inc. to Robert Bosch GmbH, 1996)
> $710 million sale of multinational automotive safety restraint business (AlliedSignal, Inc. to Breed Technologies, Inc., 1997)

> $400 million acquisition of Prestone Products Corporation (1997)
> Formation of $800 million revenue truck brake joint venture (AlliedSignal, Inc. and Knorr-Bremse AG, 1993)
> $420 milion two-step IPO and sale divestiture of oil field services company (OSCA, Inc., 2000, 2002)

Ethics compliance

> Drafted, published and circulated *Code of Business Conduct* and *Insider Trading Policy* brochures (Great Lakes Chemical, 2000, 2004).
> Designed on-line training for *Code of Business Conduct* (confidential URL available on request) (Great Lakes Chemical, 2003, 2004)

Bar membership

> Michigan (1979)
> Indiana (2001)

LEADERSHIP AND MANAGEMENT EXPERIENCE

Member of Corporate Executive Council on strategic and operating matters at Great Lakes Chemical and leader of the Law Department

> Strategic assessment and portfolio planning of a diversified $1.6 billion specialty chemical company
> Assist in drafting all earnings press releases and preparation for all CEO/CFO analyst conference calls
> Manage department of between four and six lawyers and two paralegals, and total inside-outside budget in excess of $10 million
> Instituted preferred provider outside counsel program and online cost tracking system, reducing total number of firms and the number of firms responsible for 75% of billings to six

Member of Automotive Leadership Team and Law Department Senior Staff at AlliedSignal

> Participated in strategic assessment and decision to divest automotive businesses
> Managed Automotive Law Department of up to ten general and patent lawyers
> Participated as senior staff in management of approximately 70 lawyer global law department
> Private law firm practice development and management
> Drafted and executed business plan for the Emerging Business and Technology Program, a low-cost fixed fee legal services program designed for high-potential start-up ventures that constituted the growth area of the Ann Arbor business law market

> Member, Counsel Committee (counsel to the firm on loss prevention and claims; representative of the firm to its malpractice carrier, Attorneys Liability Assurance Society, Ltd.)

COMMUNITY SERVICE

> *Park Tudor School, Indianapolis, Board of Directors (2003–present).* Pre-K through 12th grade independent private school with approximately 1,000 students.
> *Spirit & Place Festival, Indianapolis (2004).* Organized and raised funds for "Coming to Terms with Evil," lecture by Susan Neiman, director of the Einstein Forum, Berlin, and author of *Evil in Modern Thought* (co-sponsored by the Butler University Center for Faith and Vocation, Congregation Beth-El Zedeck, and Park Tudor School).
> *New Enterprise Forum, Ann Arbor, Michigan, Board of Directors (1999).* Organization supporting the entrepreneurial and venture capital community in Southeastern Michigan.

EDUCATION

Stanford University

J.D., 1979
Cartoonist, *Stanford Law Journal* (student newspaper)
Class Secretary and Correspondent

University of Michigan

A.B. in History, with High Distinction, 1975
Phi Beta Kappa
James B. Angell Scholar (two consecutive terms of all-A), 1973, 1974, 1975
Cartoonist, *Michigan Daily*

EMPLOYMENT HISTORY

Wake Forest University School of Law, Winston-Salem, North Carolina

Visiting Professor of Law, August to December 2005

Indiana University School of Law—Indianapolis

Adjunct Professor of Law, Spring Semester 2005

Great Lakes Chemical Corporation, Indianapolis, Indiana

Great Lakes was a NYSE-listed $1.6 billion global specialty chemical company with approximately 4,500 employees. It offered flame retardant and other polymer additive solutions to industrial customers, and consumer products, including recreational pool and spa and other household chemicals to wholesalers and retailers. On July 1, 2005, it merged with Crompton Corporation to become Chemtura Corporation.

> Senior Vice President, General Counsel & Secretary (October 1999 to November 2004)
> Senior Vice President & General Counsel (November 2004 to July 1, 2005) (promoted from Assistant Secretary to Vice President & Secretary)
> Interim Vice President—Corporate Development (April to December 2000)

AlliedSignal Inc., Southfield, Michigan

AlliedSignal, Inc. was an approximately $13 billion diversified multinational company, with divisions in the automotive, aerospace, and engineered materials industries (AlliedSignal later merged with and took the name Honeywell International.) Between 1992 and 1997, the automotive division ranged in size from about $6 billion down to about $3 billion, manufacturing and selling brake systems for passenger cars, light trucks, and heavy vehicles, safety restraint systems, turbochargers, filters, and spark plugs to OEM and aftermarket customers.

> Vice President & General Counsel, AlliedSignal Automotive (August 1993 to December 1997)
> Senior Counsel, AlliedSignal Automotive (October 1992 to July 1993)

Dykema Gossett, Detroit, Bloomfield Hills and Ann Arbor, Michigan

Dykema Gossett is a large law firm based in Detroit, with offices throughout Michigan, in Chicago, Los Angeles, and Washington, D.C. In the 1980s, it also operated offices in Florida, and at the time was ranked among the 100 largest law firms in the United States.

> Of Counsel, Corporate and Finance Group, Ann Arbor, Michigan (February 1998 to October 1999)
> Partner, Corporate and Finance Group, Bloomfield Hills, Michigan (August 1989 to October 1992)

Represented clients in general commercial and corporate matters, mergers and acquisitions, underwriting for conduit municipal bond financing, investment advisor registration and regulation, insurance regulation and antitrust matters, international transactions, startup and venture capital transactions.

> Partner, Litigation Group, Detroit, Michigan (April 1987 to August 1989)

Represented clients in complex commercial, antitrust, and securities litigation matters (including Rule 10b-5 and "poison pill" cases). Acted as counselor on antitrust matters, including Hart-Scott-Rodino premerger review, distribution matters, Robinson-Patman Act, and other issues. Represented different elements of the insurance industry in regulatory and marketing matters, including insolvency, rate proceedings, and marketing practices.

> Associate, Litigation Group, Detroit, Michigan (June 1979 to March 1987)

PUBLICATIONS

Freedom, Compulsion, Compliance, and Mystery: Reflections on the Duty Not to Enforce a Promise, forthcoming, LAW, CULTURE & THE HUMANITIES.

Contingency and Contracts: A Philosophy of Complex Business Transactions, forthcoming, DEPAUL L. REV.

The Bewitchment of Intelligence: Language and Ex Post Illusions of Intention, 78 TEMP. L. REV. 99 (2005).

Sarbanes-Oxley, Jurisprudence, Game Theory, Insurance and Kant: Toward a Moral Theory of Good Governance, 50 WAYNE L. REV. 1083 (2004).

Note on Judge Posner's Opinion in Lake River Corp. v. Carborundum Co., *in Teachers' Manual to* BRUCE W. FRIER & JAMES J. WHITE, THE MODERN LAW OF CONTRACTS (2005), at 26–71.

Trial, in LITIGATING THE COMMERCIAL CASE, ch. 11 (1992) (with Donald S. Young).

Appellant's Brief in *O'Dowd v. General Motors Corp.,* 4 COOLEY L. REV. 193 (1987) (Winner of the Thomas M. Cooley Law Review Distinguished Brief Award).

PROFESSIONAL PRESENTATIONS

Panelist, *NYU Journal of Law & Liberty* On-Line Symposium, "Sarbanes-Oxley and the Federalization of Corporate Law," October 28, 2005 (with Larry Ribstein, Brett McDonnell, Justice Myron Steele, Robert Ahdieh, Allen Ferrell and Larry Backer), available at http://www.nyujll.org/blog/.

Legal Aspects of Entrepreneurship, University of Michigan Business School, March 31, 1999; University of Michigan–Dearborn School of Management, March 24, 1999.

Understanding What Sellers Are Looking For, Third Auto Industry Supplier Mergers & Acquisitions Forum, Ritz-Carlton Hotel, Dearborn, Michigan, October 26, 1998.

Practicing Corporate Law, Speaker, University of Michigan Phi Alpha Delta Pre-Law Fraternity, October 6, 1998.

Year 2000 Issues, CMS Enterprises Law Department, South Haven, Michigan, September 4, 1998.

Understanding What Sellers Are Looking For, The Auto Industry Supplier Mergers & Acquisitions Forum, Hotel Nikko, Chicago, Illinois, April 14, 1997.

PERSONAL

Born: June 16, 1954. Married to Alene Franklin (Harvard College, University of Michigan, B.B.A., 1981; M.H.S.A., 1985). Children: Arielle (b.1984, attending Sarah Lawrence College), Matthew (b.1987, attending University of Michigan), James (b.1989, attending Park Tudor School).

"After": a sample academic resume created out of the same data as contained in "before" by a sympathetic law professor friend who was hoping to save the candidate some embarrassment.

Jeffrey M. Lipshaw

[Contact Information]

TEACHING EXPERIENCE

Wake Forest University School of Law, Winston-Salem, NC
Visiting Professor of Law, Fall Term, 2005
Courses: Contracts, Sales
Indiana University School of Law–Indianapolis
Adjunct Professor of Law, Spring Term, 2005
Course: Advanced Topics in Business Law: Technology Start-ups & Venture Capital

PUBLICATIONS

Freedom, Compulsion, Compliance, and Mystery: Reflections on the Duty Not to Enforce a Promise, forthcoming, LAW, CULTURE & THE HUMANITIES.

Contingency and Contracts: A Philosophy of Complex Business Transactions, forthcoming, DEPAUL L. REV.

The Bewitchment of Intelligence: Language and Ex Post Illusions of Intention, 78 TEMP. L. REV. 99 (2005).

Sarbanes-Oxley, Jurisprudence, Game Theory, Insurance and Kant: Toward a Moral Theory of Good Governance, 50 WAYNE L. REV. 1083 (2004).

Note on Judge Posner's Opinion in Lake River Corp. v. Carborundum Co., *in Teachers' Manual to* BRUCE W. FRIER & JAMES J. WHITE, THE MODERN LAW OF CONTRACTS (2005), at 268–71.

Trial, in LITIGATING THE COMMERCIAL CASE, ch. 11 (1992) (with Donald S. Young).

Appellant's Brief in *O'Dowd v. General Motors Corp.*, 4 COOLEY L. REV. 193 (1987) (Winner of the Thomas M. Cooley Law Review Distinguished Brief Award).

SELECTED PRESENTATIONS

Panelist, *NYU Journal of Law & Liberty* On-Line Symposium, "Sarbanes-Oxley and the Federalization of Corporate Law," October 28, 2005 (with Larry Ribstein, Brett McDonnell, Justice Myron Steele, Robert Ahdieh, Allen Ferrell, and Larry Backer), available at http://www.nyujll.org/blog/.

Legal Aspects of Entrepreneurship, University of Michigan Business School, March 31, 1999; University of Michigan–Dearborn School of Management, March 24, 1999.

Understanding What Sellers Are Looking For, Third Auto Industry Supplier Mergers & Acquisitions Forum, Ritz-Carlton Hotel, Dearborn, Michigan, October 26, 1998.

Practicing Corporate Law, Speaker, University of Michigan Phi Alpha Delta Pre-Law Fraternity, October 6, 1998.

Year 2000 Issues, CMS Enterprises Law Department, South Haven, Michigan, September 4, 1998.

Understanding What Sellers Are Looking For, The Auto Industry Supplier Mergers & Acquisitions Forum, Hotel Nikko, Chicago, Illinois, April 14, 1997.

SERVICE

Park Tudor School, Indianapolis, IN, Board of Directors (2003–present).

Pre-K through 12th grade independent private school with approximately 1,000 students.

Spirit & Place Festival, Indianapolis, IN (2004).

Organized and raised funds for "Coming to Terms with Evil," lecture by Susan Neiman, director of the Einstein Forum, Berlin, and author of *Evil in Modern Thought*.

New Enterprise Forum, Ann Arbor, MI, Board of Directors (1999)

Organization supporting the entrepreneurial and venture capital community in Southeastern Michigan.

EDUCATION

Stanford University

J.D., 1979

University of Michigan

A.B. in History, with High Distinction, 1975
Phi Beta Kappa
James B. Angell Scholar (two consecutive terms of all-A), 1973, 1974, 1975
Cartoonist, *Michigan Daily*

PROFESSIONAL EXPERIENCE

Great Lakes Chemical Corporation, Indianapolis, Indiana
Senior Vice President & General Counsel (1999–2005)
Interim Vice President, Corporate Development (2000)

> Overall responsibility for legal affairs of $1.6 billion, NYSE-listed global specialty chemical company with approximately 4,500 employees.

AlliedSignal Inc., Southfield, Michigan
Vice President & General Counsel, AlliedSignal Automotive (1993–1997)
Senior Counsel, AlliedSignal Automotive (1992–1993)

> Responsibility for legal affairs at $6 billion division of a $13 billion diversified multi-national company. AlliedSignal later merged with and took the name Honeywell International.

Dykema Gossett, Detroit, Bloomfield Hills and Ann Arbor, Mich.
Of Counsel, Corporate and Finance Group (1998–1999)
Partner, Corporate and Finance Group (1989–1992)
Partner, Litigation Group (1987–1989)
Associate, Litigation Group (1979–1987)

> General commercial and corporate matters, mergers and acquisitions, underwriting for conduit municipal bond financing, investment advisor registration and regulation, insurance regulation, antitrust, international transactions, startup and venture capital transactions, securities litigation, insolvency, and rate proceedings.

Bar Membership: Michigan (1979); Indiana (2001)

scholarship
  class preparation and, 111–112
  job duties and, 11–16
  women as nontraditional faculty
    candidates and, 80–81
service, job duties and, 11–16
sexual orientation/identity, 78, 84
"shepherd," 59
skills faculty
  defined, 3–4
  teaching by, 12
Social Science Research Network
  (SSRN), 2
Society of American Law Teachers
  (SALT), 90, 95
Socratic method, 12, 80, 110
Solum, Larry, 28, 33, 68–69
specialized law training, 34. *See also*
    Master of Laws (L.L.M.)
spouses, "trailing," 98
Standard Model candidates, 21–22.
    See also nontraditional faculty
    candidates
  Elite and Super-Elite, 24–25
  Non-Elite candidates, 25
  Revised, 25–26
starting rank, 96
stereotypes
  gender, 79–81
  race and, 82
  teaching/writing against stereotype, 86
summer conference expenses, 94
summer research stipend, 91, 94, 103
summertime preparation, 101, 103
Super-Elite Standard Model
  candidates, 24–25
Supreme Court case articles, 31
Supreme Court Review (University of
  Chicago Press), 31
syllabi, 12, 13, 108–109

teaching
  job duties and, 11–16
  in nontraditional areas, 86
  preparation for, 101–112
  women as nontraditional faculty
    candidates and, 80
tenure track
  credentials and, 22
  defined, 4–7

publishing by candidates, 28–29
  timelines for, 5n7, 96
  *Where Tenure Track Faculty Went to
    Law School* (Leiter), 24n8
time management, 12–13, 101–112
  casebook selection for, 104–108
  class preparation and planning
    ahead, 110–111
  course package and, 102–103
  importance of, 112
  New Law Teachers Workshop
    (AALS) for, 102, 103, 108
  pedagogy and, 109–110
  planning ahead and, 109–111
  scholarship and, 111–112
  summertime preparation, 101, 102
  syllabi and, 108–109
traits, of law professors, 17–20
"transitional" law schools, on-campus
  interviews at, 63
traveling
  for on-campus interviews, 60–61
  research and travel budgets, 92, 96

University of Chicago Law School,
  25–26, 37, 38
University of Chicago Press, 31
University of Cincinnati Law School, 37
University of Iowa Law School, 82
University of Michigan Law School, 90
University of San Diego Law School, 33
University of Wisconsin Law School, 82
"up-and-coming" law schools,
  on-campus interviews at, 62–63
U.S. News & World Report rankings,
  22, 23, 63

visiting assistant professorships
  (VAPs), 21–22, 26, 36, 37–38, 117
visiting professors, 11

Web site, as job search tool, 45–46
Wendel, Brad, 23, 29, 33
*Where Tenure Track Faculty Went to
  Law School* (Leiter), 24n8
women, as faculty candidates, 79–81

Yale Law School, 33